# The Psychology of Witnessing

Other books by Jard DeVille

*Los Buenos Tambien Ganar*
*Lovers for Life*
*Nice Guys Finish First*

# Jard DeVille
# The Psychology of Witnessing

**WORD BOOKS**
PUBLISHER
WACO, TEXAS

THE PSYCHOLOGY OF WITNESSING

ISBN 0-8499-2922-9
Library of Congress Catalog Card Number: 80-51447
*Printed in the United States of America*

*But you shall receive power when the Holy Spirit has come upon you; and you shall be my witnesses in Jerusalem, and in all Judea and Samaria and to the end of the earth.*

*Acts 1:8*

# Contents

# For the Reader

In my youth, about the time of World War II, evangelical Christianity often seemed little more than the last gasp of a dying religion. Not only had the concept of a personal encounter with God almost vanished from the churches to be replaced by an innocuous "be nice" ethic, the future of the very church itself was called into doubt by many scholars. The term "post-Christian era" was being used with increasing frequency.

As I look back at those years, I can understand why the end of the church was being predicted. Across Europe and America, Christianity had lost a great deal of its vitality. In Europe less than one person in ten paid any more than lip service to the denomination of his choice. North and south, Protestant and Catholic, Europeans were conspicuous by their absence in the cathedrals. The concepts and values of Christianity no longer had a meaningful influence on government, business or industry. In education, science had virtually become the secular religion of Western civilization. The new faith had arrived with a promise of continual progress, scientific problem solving, and a world-wide civilization in which the foibles of unsystematic politicians would be replaced by logical decisions. It seemed to many that the church had outlived its usefulness, and it was often rather lonely for those of us in the evangelical camp.

But the expected social, political and scientific miracles didn't occur. Life did not become satisfying in proportion to our increasing level of affluence. The promise of secular salvation vanished in seventy million battle deaths of this century. Along with the miracle drugs, napalm was produced; along with fast, inexpensive air travel, ballistic missiles appeared; and with miracle wheat and rice came the nuclear bombs which have the destructive force to crush civilization into a stone-age desert. The more life changed, the more complex the problems became.

Millions of Americans and Europeans now feel trapped in existential alienation and frustration, until alcoholism, divorce, depression and suicide have become common. Human rights are vanishing as nation after nation turns to totalitarianism to solve their continuing problems which seem to have no solutions. Our cities, the centers of civilization for all nations, are crumbling into decay and violence as our problems mount—despite the spending of billions of dollars to save them. The fact of the matter is that neither science nor politics, alone or in combination, can change hearts and minds to live in love, mutual acceptance and hope, rather than in hate and despair. Secular salvation remains the myth that it always has been.

As a result of our slowly awakening knowledge, perceptive men and women from all walks of life are realizing that the gospel of Christ has a timeless quality about it. Each person has a spiritual unconscious which much be satisfied, or life cannot become fulfilling. Our ancestors called this the God-ache within the human heart. Of course, as long ago as 1850, Sören Kierkegaard had written that only in a self-transcending faith in God can humankind survive the pressures of our era. We have had to rediscover this for ourselves, for any civilization which tries to be sufficient unto itself without God eventually becomes spiritually bankrupt.

The only hope I see for individuals or nations is found in a self-transcending relationship with God in the Lord Jesus Christ. This relationship allows us to apply our scientific and social knowledge in ways which are not self-defeating. A great many other folk feel the same way, evidently. Some 35 percent or more of American adults report that they have had a personal encounter with Christ which has a major influence on their values, attitudes, expectations and choices. For an evangelical from the skeptical '30s and '40s, this is marvelous, indeed. Recently I had breakfast with a businessman to discuss a possible joint venture; and before we had finished talking, he had found a way to share his faith with me. I responded, and the business meeting became a spiritual fellowship right in the restaurant. And that is no longer the uncommon experience it was in my youth.

There is a growing awareness that fulfillment can come only in Christian commitment. In our opportunities to witness and lead others to Christ, love must be channeled purposefully if it is to be effective. I have found that the methods I teach here and in my *Sharing the Faith* seminars can be used to excellent advantage when you witness in love and compassion. I know of no other place you can learn them, except through a long trial and error process which will leave you discouraged and others confused. I

pray that you will use them to become the best possible
witness for Christ. Share the faith often, for there are
millions who need it right now!

As far as my own testimony, Charles Wesley, the poet
laureate of Methodism, stated it much better than I can. He
wrote as I wish that I could:

> And can it be that I should gain
> An interest in the Saviour's blood?
> Died he for me, who caused his pain?
> For me, who him to death pursued?
> Amazing love! how can it be
> That thou, my Lord, shouldst die for me?
>
> 'Tis mystery all! the Immortal dies!
> Who can explore his strange design?
> In vain the firstborn seraph tries
> To sound the depths of love divine.
> 'Tis mercy all! let earth adore:
> Let angel minds inquire no more.
>
> Long my imprisoned spirit lay,
> Fast bound in sin and nature's night;
> Thine eye diffused a quickening ray;
> I woke, the dungeon flamed with light:
> My chains fell off, my heart was free,
> I rose, went forth, and followed thee.
>
> No condemnation now I dread,
> Jesus, with all in him, is mine:
> Alive in him, my living Head,
> And clothed in righteousness divine,
> Bold I approach the eternal throne
> And claim the crown, through Christ my own.

*Jard DeVille*
Minneapolis, 1980

——————————One ——————————

# Personal Responsibility

The responsibility of every committed Christian to lovingly lead other men and women to a personal relationship with the Lord Jesus Christ and to fellowship and service in the church was carefully spelled out in the great commission.

Go therefore and make disciples of all nations, baptizing them in the name of the Father and of the Son and of the Holy Spirit, teaching them to observe all that I have commanded you (Matt. 28:19,20).

The crucial work of personal evangelism can only be successful under the leadership of the Holy Spirit. But each Christian has talents and gifts that can be applied with loving concern when the divine *and* human combine in the task of winning men and women to Christ. To lead others to this wise decision, we must remain consistently compassionate as we share the joy and satisfaction that being in Christ makes possible for us. To help in this greatest of all spiritual activities, we can learn to use some psycho-spiritually sound methods which are consistent with the love, acceptance and freedom of choice that Jesus always granted to men and women. As we accept Jesus' commission, we can enhance our effectiveness by learning several specific skills to structure our love and concern under the leadership of the Holy Spirit.

*Who Should Witness?*

As I conduct my *Sharing the Faith* seminars, I've become convinced that most Christian men and women want to share their self-transcending Christian experiences with the people they know and love. The growth of the relational Christian movement during the last two decades or so is just the tip of a gigantic iceberg of what is happening within the church. Throughout Christianity a massive stirring is taking place as people are becoming increasingly aware that a personal commitment to Christ is both theologically and psychologically sound.

In this ever-growing fellowship with Christ, many men and women want to share their joyous Christian faith with the people they know. Perhaps you are in this group. Yet, because some Christians do not know how to proceed in leading others to Christ, many have fallen short of fulfilling Jesus' commission to witness in their personal circles. Some begin to witness, fail, become too discouraged to try again, and feel deep guilt about their failure.

I certainly have no intention of creating any more guilt for anyone in this approach to personal evangelism, for neither you nor I need that. I simply want to share with you some of the methods I discovered most effective for me as I witnessed in the different pastorates I held, in the colleges where I taught psychology, and in the clinics where I worked and administered the programs. If you realize that the great commission was for you, even if you need help in becoming a more excellent fisher of men and women, these methods will prove invaluable. If you are unsure about your ability to testify, you will find this book offers the kind of structure a beginner often needs to keep from floundering about and becoming discouraged. It seems that some are born anew as fishers of men, while others have to learn some techniques before they are effective. I suspect that this is the result of personality patterns rather than a reflection of one's commitment or lack of it.

The processes and methods taught in *The Psychology of Witnessing,* as well as in my seminars for the churches, are designed to help witnesses *in conjunction* with the leading of the Holy Spirit. And while the Spirit is necessary, I insist that very little is ever accomplished in any area of religious service unless humans begin and complete tasks with love *and* labor. Leading others to Christ and the church, like constructing church buildings, starting mission congregations, and paying for inner-city programs, is *always* a combination of human and divine effort. When men and women fail to complete their part of the divine/human interaction, little is accomplished and the church is crippled.

The methods I teach do not form a presentation like a salesman might make in selling a product to a customer. Neither are they a subtle form of manipulation. Rather, they are in the format that a psychologist or psychiatrist often uses to help a client discover both his problems *and* what will enable him to live a satisfying life. They include understanding, acceptance and mutual discovery, as well as a number of other emotions. The skills are the human elements I find necessary in the divine/human effort of winning people to Christ. Obviously, I cannot predict the moving of the Holy Spirit in opening opportunities for you to tell your story of spiritual rebirth with love and compassion. Neither can I know that you will study the Scriptures and pray in preparing to be a more effective witness. That will have to remain between God and you. But I can offer you some powerful psychospiritual concepts and the opportunity to master some methods which can be applied under the leading of the Holy Spirit as you follow Jesus' injunction to witness. Incidentally, I see no more lack of faith in learning these methods than I see in a young man or woman attending seminary to become a better pastor.

It is obvious that these skills should never be used to manipulate other people emotionally. They are offered with the assumption that in Christ you will respect the integrity and freedom of men and women to make their choices in a valid manner. Using the methods in a less than honorable manner would reveal a lack of respect for the other person, as well as a lack of faith in God to do his part in your enterprise for souls. On a purely practical level, such a practice will usually backfire since we can all interpret discrepancies that exist between saying one thing and believing something else. We send out two sets of signals, verbal and nonverbal, and since we learn nonverbal messages before we learn to talk, nonverbal signals are usually the most meaningful ones.

When sound psychospiritual methods are used supportively rather than manipulatively, they will allow you to reduce suspicion, to develop warm relationships quickly, and to consistently be a good witness for Christ. They are not "gimmicks" to be used in playing a role, but are rather some practical ways of sharing your love, knowledge, concern and wisdom about spiritual matters.

*People Are Fearful*

Many men and women are suspicious of those who witness to them about spiritual needs. They often feel that their religious beliefs are their own business and no concern of others. Some people have been so manipulated by religious hustlers who believe the ends justify the means they use, that they need time to accept you into their private existence of pain, joy, fear, hope and happiness. No one wants to become vulnerable to others, and in a sense this is what we are asking others to do in committing their lives to Christ. Normally, you will have to reduce another person's fears before he will listen to your witness.

One exception to this may be strangers who will sometimes discuss spiritual needs freely since they know they will be leaving you in a short while. At such times a supportive word of testimony can be effective. Most of the time, however, you will have to "pay your dues" in love and support before you earn the right to witness to another person. You will have to invest enough time and understanding to enter his private world, as only a friend can do, before he will really hear what you are saying about committing himself to Christ and the church.

People *are* hopeful, however. They do want to believe that your testimony is true, that a way of life which is filled with satisfaction and happiness can be found. Underneath his doubts and fears of being hurt once more, the most cynical person hopes that you know something real to help him ease the pain of living a spiritually bankrupt life. But in virtually all cases you will have to commit enough of your love and compassion to become a friend before you can convince someone what a commitment to Christ can accomplish. Your *example* is much better than your *story*, of course. And a prime example of that is the story of Kenny

Jones. After all, few people know Kenny Jones like I did. Kenny was an old-time gangster right out of the movies, as badly hooked by heroin as anyone I have ever known. I met him when I came back from the Army to college at Pasadena, California. He had been shooting heroin for twenty-three years when some kids from the college found him holed-up in a cottage near the school. They went to him with the message of deliverance; but he cursed them, the college and God. They persisted in their expression of support and love until, beneath his street toughness, he began to hope and pray that they knew *something* he didn't. When they continued to love him with a no-nonsense, tough love that challenged him to test God, he finally discovered that they did know *someone* he did not know. Kenny spent about thirty minutes in prayer one evening, making a commitment of his life to Christ, a commitment which so revolutionized his life that he went off heroin *cold turkey* in that same half hour. It was such a spiritual rebirth that he did not even experience withdrawal symptoms, and I can document that for any skeptics!

Such a self-transforming encounter with the personal Christ is by no means a rare experience. From Saul of Tarsus to Charles Colson of Watergate notoriety, kings, day laborers, soldiers, housewives, psychiatrists, presidents and people from all walks of life have testified to having encountered God through Christ. With Saul the encounter was violent enough to crush and blind him. With the kindly Albert Schweitzer it was the growing realization that his music was not enough service to offer. He went to Africa and the edge of civilization to help men and women for Christ.

It is not our responsibility to dictate the conditions through which the Holy Spirit reaches people. Rather, our task, as we express our love in different ways, is to witness in such a way that our friends can feel our concern for them and see our wisdom in recommending that they commit their lives to Christ.

*Progression in Friendship*
To be effective in establishing the kind of relationship which causes people to listen seriously when you talk about spiritual matters, you can follow a progression which captures their interest. The three steps of the progression are:

I. *Relating in Love and Compassion*
II. *Recognizing How They See Their Needs*
III. *Recommending a Solution Which Makes Sense*

As you witness to another person, you should be in one of these postures at all times. You will have to shift from one to another as circumstances change, but this is the basic framework from which you should work in winning first a friend and then a brother or sister in Christ.

The *first step*, relating warmly and sincerely enough to establish a solid friendship, is necessary for two reasons. First of all, it keeps you from becoming manipulative and confusing the ends with the means. I sincerely hope that no one uses these concepts for manipulative purposes, since I so hate being used or manipulated myself. That would be an insult to the recipient, as well as distrust of the Holy Spirit. Second, by structuring the relationship with the psychospiritual methods I teach, you enable others to lower their defenses and to see you as a caring friend without fear of being hurt.

Over a period of some twenty-five years I have conducted more than 5,000 hours of psychotherapy and counseling with people who had all kinds of emotional disorders. In that time I did not meet a single person who did not want to be treated as a friend and share warm relationships with trusted people. Unfortunately, some of these people had been so badly hurt by others that they formed a shell to protect themselves from additional pain. But behind the façade was a longing to be met with love and respect.

Years ago Harry Stack Sullivan had been hired as the Director of Wooster State Hospital for the mentally ill. In making his rounds for the first time with his staff, he saw a poor man who had been motionless in a catatonic state for months. He asked his doctors about the man and was told that the case was hopeless, that the patient had received all the treatment the hospital could give with no results. Sullivan looked at the sufferer for a few minutes without speaking and then drew a chair to the bedside.

He sat motionless with the catatonic man for a short time and then reached out to take the unresisting hand. He held it and caressed it for a while, and then the world-famous psychiatrist started to weep. As he sobbed, he said, "It's so hard. It's so hard, isn't it, my friend?" And to the amazement of the staff who had been doing things *for* the man but not *with* him, the patient, who had neither moved nor spoken in months, turned his head toward Sullivan and told him that life was indeed too painful to bear at times. Instead of talking down to him as the other *experts* had done, Sullivan empathetically felt the man's pain and related to him as a caring friend, as we must do in our witnessing.

The *second step* in the relationship we must establish is that of getting into your friend's personal world, since no two people, even in the same family, have the same genes and experiences. You cannot hope to convince anyone if you focus your testimony on something he does not yet understand. People simply do not hear our answers to questions they have not yet asked for themselves. A canned presentation that is directed toward some hypothetically average person may be like trying to sell tickets on the Ark to someone who had been praying for rain for two years! *You* know that Christ offers the love and faith needed to make life rich and full, but unless you can discover the other person's needs and direct the gospel message specifically toward meeting them, you are operating in a hit-or-miss fashion. I realize that the Holy Spirit will bless what you do, but working with knowledge is as important here as it is in designing a sanctuary so it will be acoustically pleasant.

Not long ago I received several visits from a man who came to my home to recommend *his* solution to *my* spiritual needs. From the time he started talking until the time he left, he never once asked whether I had any needs I wanted to meet. He assumed that he knew what I needed, but he was all wrong. When he found out that I wrote for religious publications, he really intensified his attempts to sell me his form of worship, bringing other people in who would be even more convincing. When he paused long enough for me to tell him that I had committed my life to Christ and was living with the joy of the Lord in my heart, he immediately informed me that I was following a delusion that would exclude me from Jehovah's Kingdom. When I witnessed to him, he stormed out of the house, telling me that he had delivered his soul, had done his duty, and my blood was on my own head. I sensed none of the love and compassion of Christ in the series of visits. He certainly made no effort to find out what I needed in the relationship, so I felt no obligation to listen seriously to him.

Until we *relate* warmly and *recognize* a friend's needs as
he sees them, we don't have enough knowledge to picture
the gospel in the light that will be most attractive to him.
We have not *earned the right* to ask him to commit his life to
Christ as a means of meeting his spiritual needs! In a
majority of cases we will be firing in the dark and expecting
the Holy Spirit to do more than his share of the work.
Perhaps we will even be hindering the Spirit's work.

After you have learned what your friend perceives as his
problems and needs in life *and* have lovingly supported
him in the relationship, you are then in a position to
*recommend* a solution to life's problems that will capture his
interest. You will probably not be successful in recommending Christ as a source of peace and tranquillity to a
young athlete who is striving for all-conference football
honors. Neither will you be too helpful in recommending
Christ as a means of improving creativity and productivity
to an elderly woman in a nursing home. Both people need
a personal relationship with Christ, but each one's interest
will have to be captured initially in a completely different
way.

Be realistic and honest as you recommend solutions in
Christ. Promising too much too quickly can only lead to
frustration and disappointment and discredit your testimony. Most men and women are perceptive enough to
recognize that becoming a Christian will not solve all their
problems without much hard work. Giving one's life to
Christ does not end all divorces, stop all business failures,
keep people from losing their jobs, or guarantee success in
the professions, though I've heard immature people say
that.

Neither a physician nor a psychotherapist recommends a
solution before he finds the cause of each person's illness.
He knows that something is out of order, of course; but

that is not specific enough. Your recommendation should fit as closely as possible the symptoms of spiritual bankruptcy he has become aware of, for that is the most likely place where the Holy Spirit will deal with him.

One of the most effective Christian lay witnesses I have ever known is a professor at a large state university. Daniel is a powerful man of enormous prestige as both a researcher and a teacher. He is respected by his colleagues and adored by the students. Each year, soon after classes start in the fall, he focuses his prayer and concern on a number of students to whom the Holy Spirit seems to be directing him.

Dan woos them as his friends, asking them to take part in his experiments and writing, inviting them to his home for dinner, and overseeing their projects. While he does not neglect either his responsibilities to the department or the other students, he does build supportive relationships with these special youngsters and searches out as much as he can about their needs. Only then does he start sharing with them the secret of his full, influential life, telling them about the Christ who is at the center of his existence. Over the years, kneeling by the fireplace in his study, or seated in his office, he has led hundreds of the finest young men and women on that campus to commit their lives to Christ and service in the church. Without consciously thinking it through, my friend Dan is doing what I have found to be needed in the progression I've presented here.

Some people get the cart before the horse in their witnessing. They ask God to give them a burden for souls before they start sharing the good news of Christ. Unfortunately, as any psychologist knows, life seldom moves in that manner. Psychological research reveals that a person can *act* himself into a new way of thinking much faster than he can *think* himself into a different way of behaving. My point is that you can do very little witnessing in a cave or a monastery. You must begin by sharing your faith with the people whose trust you already have, the people around you who are in physical, psychological and spiritual need. Then, as you start relating more deeply in love, your concern for others will increase; and you will find that God has started to point out more and more people for you to witness to.

## KEY CONCEPTS FROM CHAPTER ONE

1. All Christians are called to invest their lives in obeying the great commission of Christ.
2. Christian commitment can come like a bolt of lightning or be gradual as one meets with Christ.
3. It is easier to act oneself into a new way of feeling than to think oneself into a new way of behaving.
4. The progression to leading a friend to Christ includes:
   *relating* in love and support,
   *recognizing* his needs as he sees them,
   *recommending* a solution that makes sense to him.

## KEY QUESTIONS TO ASK YOURSELF

1. Am I accepting my responsibility to witness as best I can?
2. Have I convinced myself that soul-winning is the responsibility of only a few in the church?
3. Am I willing to give enough of myself to become supportive of others?
4. Will I learn and follow the progression of relating, recognizing and recommending as one good friend will do for another in many areas of life?

# Two

# Personal Maturity

Each person who attempts the loving task of soul-winning as part of his Christian worship is working from one of four states of effectiveness. These four states are:

*Unconsciously Ineffective*
*Consciously Ineffective*
*Unconsciously Effective*
*Consciously Effective*

If you are *unconsciously ineffective* you do not understand how to influence the people you know to commit their lives to Christ; and worse, you do not know how inadequate your skills are. You have no incentive to improve. Many of the men and women who are like the insensitive man I wrote about in the preceding chapter work from this orientation. They assume that their spiel is effective and that people are rejecting their advice because of misplaced or sinister motives. Such a person may be unteachable.

A witness who is *consciously ineffective* is in a better position because he at least realizes he does not know what is effective and what is not. If he will learn the skills necessary, spend time in prayer, and study the Scriptures, he can grow beyond his present limitations.

Still better off is the *unconsciously effective* person; for he is able to get into the framework of the people to whom he witnesses and influence their decisions at times, providing he doesn't encounter fear or resistance. Then his lack of understanding about successful persuasion becomes a hindrance, for he does not know what he is doing that is different from his successful experiences.

The most competent witness of all is the *consciously effective* soul-winner. Such a person knows why he has been successful and why he has failed. He knows when he has done all he can and if the refusal was the result of factors he could not control—such as the free choice of the person with whom he was dealing. With his knowledge *and* wisdom, he is prepared to move through any door, in love and support, that the Holy Spirit opens to him. If the Holy Spirit is still dealing with his friend, he can bide his time patiently, trusting that God is even more interested in the outcome than he and that he can make an opportunity to deal with his friend at a better time in the future.

I sincerely hope that with the help I'm offering as best I know how, you will become a consciously effective witness to the grace, love and joy of the Lord Jesus Christ, for I believe that there is no higher calling for any of us who love him. I see three crucial characteristics in the character of each man or woman who attempts to take part in this loving enterprise for the good of humankind: strong spiritual values, emotional honesty, and harnessed creativity.

*Spiritual Values*

Each person lives with a value system which determines the attitudes, expectations and activities of his life. If the system is strong because of its spirituality, a man or woman can live according to eternal principles, rather than by a series of expedient shortcuts which are valuable at the moment but are eventually destructive. Frustrated, unhappy people often fall into the trap of living for the moment alone. They have few long-term goals, or else lose sight of them when the pressures of a spiritually bankrupt life grow worse.

A strong value system which is rooted in Christian love has four dimensions to it. They are cosmic, creative, experiential and attitudinal in nature. In a person's life they can look like this:

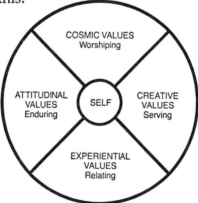

*Cosmic* values are expressed in a person's life by *worshiping* in the Lord Jesus Christ. I see this as the keystone of one's personal value system. Through worshiping sincerely you relate yourself to the eternal principles of life and love as personified by Jesus. Cosmic values give us a sense of permanence which endures past the unstable, fast-changing aspects of our short lives. Worship is the mortar which holds the entire structure of a person's value system together successfully.

*Creative* values are expressed practically by *serving* humankind loyally with a life task or a mission of some kind. In thousands of hours of conducting therapy with people from all walks of life I have found that men and women really need to give of themselves to society in a specific way. Even Eric Hoffer, the longshoreman/philoso- pher who is not a Christian author by any means, wrote that the need to be useful is more important than being affluent, or even politically free. Each person needs a job to do which will not be done, or at least will not be done as well, if he or she did not do it. This task may be the way in which he earns a living, or it may be an avocation through which he finds a means of helping other people because he loves them.

*Experiential* values are made effective in each person's life by *relating* in love and friendship to the people who give a sense of community to his existence. This is what you take from society after you have identified with God and given of yourself in service. For your own mental and spiritual health you need to live in love with the people who are important to you, with the people from whom you want nothing but affection and support. Of course, as a com- mitted Christian witness, you will also be able to benefit from the relationships you develop as a means of opening doors through which to testify.

The final set of values in a spiritual value system are the *attitudinal* values which are expressed by *enduring* bravely the inevitable painful aspects of life. In doing this you respond realistically to life as a good soldier in Christ, for life is not a rose garden, but interspaced with pain, guilt and death for each of us. I am selfish enough to wish that my personal commitment to Christ would remove all pain from my life, but it has not; and pretending that it has is a self-deception which would only limit my ability to relate to others who have accepted reality as it is. I have been ill as you have, needed an operation, had disappointments in life, seen my mother sicken and die, and lived through a world war that took many of my friends in their youth. Such pain must be endured in faith, for neither science nor religion is going to change the fact that humans are born to trouble as certainly as the sparks of a campfire fly upward, as stated in Job long ago. A commitment to Christ certainly softens the blows of life, but it does not end them; and though we weep, we do not grieve as those who have no hope.

We must draw from the strengths of a Christian value system as we mature in love and concern for others. In speaking about maturity, I do not feel that it is appropriate for a Christian to think in terms of his being good or bad, smart or stupid. Certainly, Christ's sacrifice and resurrection took care of the good or bad concept for all those who abide in him, imparting to Christians the very strengths of God's own nature. Of course I see a qualitative difference, but as a bucket of sea water can contain all the elements of the sea without having any of its tempestuous power, so a Christian shows traces of God's nature without having his majesty and holiness.

As loving men and women who care enough about others to want to testify to them, we need to ask ourselves whether we are interacting with them maturely as we grow in grace. Or have we remained spiritual infants who expect to be petted and coddled, lest we become petulant with the people we should be helping?

There is little value in confusing maturity with being redeemed, either. Our relationship and standing with God comes as a result of his divine grace and love when he accepts us into his family. Maturity comes more gradually, as a result of living spiritually through good times and bad, operating with strong Christian values, and making responsible, character-building choices. It takes time for a person to mature, but we must help ourselves along the way by living according to our best knowledge after our initial encounter with Christ.

Not long after Charles Colson was led to the Lord, I heard him speak at a conference. He was chain-smoking at the time and using a vocabulary which was still rooted in his "walk over his grandmother to help the president" days. I had no doubt about his self-transcending experience with Christ, but on the other hand, no one present could consider him a mature, exemplary Christian either. I recently heard him speak again, and the growth he revealed is impressive. He is still a driving, impatient, man, but he has matured a great deal. It takes time and effort to mature, and we should expect that in dealing with the people we are leading to the Lord. However, the more spiritual a person's values are, the faster he will grow in grace and love.

*Emotional Honesty*

From time to time in my counseling I hear Christians bemoan the fact that God did not remove their old feelings when they committed their lives to Christ. They seem to believe that life would be much happier, regardless of the circumstances, if they did not have to cope with their emotions. Actually, our full range of feelings is one of the qualities which separates us from the lower animals; and they all should be treasured. If a person is not comfortable with the things he or she feels, however, a number of problems can be created when he attempts to witness. It is disastrous to pretend to feel one emotion while actually experiencing something else.

One research study revealed that only 7 percent of our interpersonal communication is spoken aloud.* Thirty-eight percent is communicated by body language, and 55 percent is conveyed by tone of voice. Because of discrepancies between that 7 percent and the other 93 percent, each infant learns to interpret nonverbal communication long before he can understand words. Because of this earlier learning and the fact that nonverbal communication is more basic to our feelings, any difference between what is verbalized and what is expressed nonverbally is quickly detected by most people. Nonverbal messages are much more convincing to us.

For example, a woman who states quietly that she doesn't mind waiting in line at a store, while at the same time her teeth are clenched and her eyes are flashing sparks, is sending one message with her words and another with her body to the luckless salesperson. He can see the difference and may spend so much time and energy watching her that he makes a mistake with her order. The salesman may not be able to escape from her or her contradictory messages. But when you are witnessing, you are not likely to have a captive audience. If you are distraught enough to say one thing verbally and another nonverbally, your friend will very likely reach one of two conclusions about you. He may decide that you are losing control of yourself and do not know what is happening to you. In that case, he may decide to get out of the way before he gets hit by the flying parts. On the other hand, he may assume that you are deliberately lying as a means

---

*David Augsburger and John Faul, *Beyond Assertiveness* (Waco, TX: Word Books, Publisher, 1980).

of setting him up for your own benefit. He may feel that he has caught a glimpse of the real you through a flaw in your mask. In that case you have also lost your influence over him, for who wants to be deliberately deceived for whatever reason?

Carl Rogers, the dean of American psychologists and a man of strong spiritual values, calls on us to be *authentic* with each other as a means of improving our interpersonal communication. He wrote that an authentic person is free enough from psychological repression to recognize his own emotions, even when they are anger or fear or some other supposed baser feeling. He is also able to accept the fact that all feelings are legitimate in themselves and necessary for us to live successfully. Finally, an authentic, or emotionally honest, person is willing, when it is appropriate, to share his feelings with others.

Some years ago, when I was chairman of a college psychology department, I attended a divisional meeting of the departmental chairmen. The college was in a financial crisis, and each chairman arrived with his or her fears of what would happen to his program in years to come. Since we were generally reasonable Christian men and women, we soon reached the conclusion that we would have to bite the bullet together, that no one would be sacrificed so all the other programs could go on unchanged. That was the easy part, for we next had to decide what would be trimmed from each budget in a manner fair to everyone. A great deal of hard bargaining followed, with much give and take.

As the negotiations grew complex, one chairman became more and more disturbed by what was happening. He was the one determined to surrender nothing, regardless of what happened to the rest of us. Consequently, virtually every defensive move of his was voted down with little or no discussion, for we knew his motives in advance. In time his face grew red, his breathing more rapid, and his remarks more personal. It was obvious to everyone in the room that the man was furious, but we said nothing to him about his emotions.

Finally, the longsuffering divisional chairman chided him gently: "Tom, don't take this so personally. Just because we all have to sacrifice something, you don't have to become so angry."

I'll never forget Tom's reaction. The red-faced man lunged wildly to his feet, knocked his chair across the room, pounded both fists on the table, and shouted, *"I am not angry!"*

He was genuinely surprised and deeply offended when the entire group of his peers broke up in near hysterical laughter at his statement. Not only was he furious, but he was totally ignorant of the fact that he was sending contradictory messages. And because he could not recognize what his feelings were, he was unable to contribute to the decisions which were to affect his department for years to come. Because he was defensive, we were also; and no one was willing to give him any extra money for his department.

I avoid confusing people by checking on my feelings from time to time when I am talking to them about important matters. For there is a deep hidden stratum of emotions that St. Paul called the carnal nature (Freud called it the id) in our minds. It can cause conflicts which make little or no sense after they are resolved. I certainly don't want to confuse anyone I'm witnessing to by saying one thing and conveying a totally different message at a more primitive level. I want my friend to give me his total attention, rather than focusing on self-protection because I am emotionally dishonest with him. If I feel distressed by something that happened earlier, angry because of job pressures, frightened because I have just missed getting hit on the freeway, or resentful of something, I will not talk to my friend about spiritual matters. I do find that prayer helps me get beyond temporary negative feelings; but in most cases I still wait for a better time, unless there are special circumstances.

Virtually everyone will accept your right to your own feelings. They may not be willing to accept psychological games or verbal assaults so you can gain emotional relief at their expense; but if you are not causing them pain, they will most often accept your feelings as legitimate.

Jesus was certainly authentic about his feelings. The scribes and Pharisees felt his scorn when they pretended to be the guardians of God's love. The moneychangers in the temple fled from his wrath when they were dishonoring the house of his Father. And in the garden, before he was arrested, Jesus suffered nothing less than an anxiety attack as he came to grips with the fact of his coming death. He overcame his attack and went on with his divine duty, of course; but he felt the same emotions we do and was able to recognize and cope with them in ways which were not destructive. And we must also, if we want to lead our friends to commit their lives to him.

*Harnessed Creativity*

In becoming a consistently effective witness for Christ, you'll need to draw deeply from your faith, turn your restored imagination over to God, and press your personal ministry past the conventional limits. Be willing to go beyond the concepts of your parents and grandparents, for twentieth-century men and women, enjoying the fruits of and suffering the alienation of our affluent age, are not often captivated by answers and solutions to their ancestors' problems. They expect answers that make sense in the only life style they have ever known in this fastest changing of all ages.

Even Christians who find purpose and permanence in Christ sometimes remain confused by the events which are sweeping over us faster than we can interpret them, but we need not be afraid. Life styles, products and relationships are changing without a doubt; but by abiding in Christ we have a stability from which we can allow change to come and go without sacrificing the inner core of who we are. I find that the renewal of relational Christianity is not a return to the past, as some people have assumed because they are uncomfortable with the changes now taking place in society. Rather, it is this generation's interpretation of the gospel message for its own time and in its own way. This is not looking back, but pressing on toward maturity.

I find nothing more crippling to a sincere Christian's testimony than his clinging desperately to the past because of his fears of the present and future. This stifles his God-given creativity to challenge life anew with knowledge and skills that are suited for this generation. In short, I don't want anything to come between me and others as I share the love and hope that being in Christ brings to people of all classes and ages despite the confusion and conflicts of our time.

To prosper rather than simply hang on in this age, Alvin Toffler suggested that each person needs to pack a survival kit. In his book *Future Shock*, Toffler made a good case that our greatest emotional villain is change itself, change that sweeps over us at the speed with which a kaleidoscope changes its images. Like the child's toy, our experiences no sooner become routine and comfortable than they flash into a new mode, and we have to adjust once more.

Therefore, people who do not keep the permanence of God at the core of their being never really feel at home in life. The love and spiritual stability that God offers us as the key to living at peace with ourselves and our world is missing. Toffler wrote, very perceptively I feel, that a personal survival kit in this day and age contains three items which we all need. And while he did not make the spiritual application that I feel I must share, they are nonetheless valid for Christians who want to mature enough to become better witnesses to the peace of God. The three skills needed for psychospiritual survival are:

*Learning to Learn*
*Learning to Choose*
*Learning to Relate*

The time has passed, along with the town pump, the water wheel and the circuit-riding preacher, when men and women were forced to choose between faith and knowledge, between religion and science. That division is no longer viable, for the further science progresses past the simplistic mechanistic concepts of Newton into wave theory, the quantum mechanics and multiple universes with black holes being the doors between them, the smaller the differences between matter and spirit become.

The knowledge explosion which started with the development of moveable type that led to printing has not yet peaked, since learning is now showing signs of being captured by electronic means. Just studying routinely in school memorizing facts by rote is largely worthless, though it continues since most people grew up with that in the past. As a Christian who has spent much of his adult life in education, I know that teaching students to use laborious calculations, square root processes and logarithms is largely useless when ten dollars will buy a calculator that will do any math that 99 percent of the people on earth will ever have to do. In other words, no child or adult can learn what he needs to know while in school, because knowledge is expanding faster than any one person can comprehend—in virtually all fields. And the fact of the matter is that if you have not studied endlessly in your own field for twenty years or so, you are hopelessly behind; for knowledge is doubling every seven years.

Since more than 90 percent of all scientists who have ever lived are alive and working today, you need to learn how to find what you need to know when you need it rather than when you are in school. You must use journals, libraries, data storage systems, and whatever the future is going to offer as you *learn to learn.*

For example, my hobby is designing and building full-size aircraft. I am currently building a family plane to carry two adults and three children at two hundred miles per hour for a thousand miles between fuel stops. I intend that the plane be built at home by an amateur builder for the cost of building a weekend sailboat. Just five years ago this plane would have been an impossibility, for the fiberglass and styrofoam materials and techniques had not yet been developed. Nothing that a student engineer studied in design school twenty years ago would have prepared him for these simple, fast-construction techniques. It took the development of space-age materials to make my plane possible. Yet, by learning to learn what I need at the present, I have come up with an aircraft which is completely unique in design, appearance and simplicity.

In addition to learning to learn, each Christian who

wants to be at his best must *learn to choose* wisely, more or
less continually. Today you have more demands made
upon you, more opportunities in which to invest your time
and money, than an emperor had just a hundred years
ago. Spend an evening leafing through several maga-
zines or watch television advertisements to see the vari-
ety of products which were not available just a decade
ago.

My son is a senior in high school this year, and he is
being bombarded by a barrage of brochures and catalogues
from colleges and technical schools from Maine to California. Just a few decades ago a youngster in his position had
relatively few occupations from which to choose. Today,
my son can choose from more than twenty thousand
occupations and professions! He, like all of us, needs to
develop a procedure for evaluating the importance of the
things which are clamoring for his time and interest, or else
he'll be overwhelmed by the products, people and plea-
sures which are continually bidding for his attention. By
learning to choose according to your Christian values,
you'll not be shifting from one goal to another as the
intensity and frequency of the demands change, but rather
remaining steady and sure of yourself.

Finally, you must *learn to relate* well to others in a world
that has become a crowded place for most of us. More than
25 percent of all humans who have ever lived are alive on
earth as you read this paragraph. They are not necessarily
well, for some 75 percent of them have major problems
with food and health care; and the problem is going to get
much worse before it is resolved.

In the meantime, with all these men and women
crowded into cities, competing for space, jobs and comfort,
rubbing each other's nerves raw, the old "grab-what-you-

can" gunfighter approach used by the human race for so long is disastrous. It is sure to cause conflict and pain, for an immutable psychospiritual law, first taught by Jesus, is that "like begets like" in human activities. The way we treat other people is the way they will treat us.

Just recently I was called in to mediate a conflict between a young wife and her husband whose marriage was coming apart. In their hurt and anger they were using their four-year-old daughter as a pawn to strike out at each other. I arrived on the scene to find the mother and her mother-in-law literally pulling the child in opposite directions by her arms. The women were screaming, and the child was crying—so I took her from them and walked away to sit alone with her, calming her in a corner of the garden

Her sobbing soon stopped as we sat with our backs to the confrontation still continuing in the yard. As we sat there, the child's father arrived in a furious rage. He swore at both the women and literally ran over to me, demanding his child. I stood up and walked to meet him, asking if he was ready to love her or whether she was a chip in his game to defeat his wife. I spoke calmly and kindly, and he reacted as I first treated him. The anger in his face passed, so I hugged her and handed her to him. I told him that I thought he had too much love for her to cause any more fear and pain. He hugged her close for a moment and then went to his wife and suggested they go off alone with the child to settle their dispute.

What I did with him was not accidental. I knew precisely what I was doing in hugging his daughter and kissing her just before I handed her to him. And he could do no less than his friend had done. I had hooked his mature, problem-solving ability by remaining apart from the quarreling women and demonstrating my concern for his daughter.

Some people may call this manipulation, but I reject that, for I do not believe that we must allow human nature to run its course regardless when we have the love and knowledge to change the outcome. Using our skills to lead others to Christ is in the same category as a teacher making math interesting with skill games, a pastor using illustrations to add interest to his evangelistic sermons, and a physician harnessing his bedside manner to keep a person involved in his own healing process. It is simply a way of learning to relate in a way that is somewhat more structured toward a worthwhile goal than we normally use in our interpersonal relationships.

KEY CONCEPTS FROM CHAPTER TWO

1.  The four aspects of a spiritual, deeply loving value system include cosmic values, creative values, experiential values and attitudinal values.
2.  Being authentic or emotionally honest means that you can recognize your own feelings, accept them as legitimate, and share them with others when appropriate.
3.  Toffler's survival kit that Christians can adapt to be more effective witnesses includes Learning to Learn, Learning to Choose and Learning to Relate.

KEY QUESTIONS TO ASK YOURSELF

1.  Am I living with strong spiritual values which combine worshiping in Christ, serving faithfully, relating warmly and enduring bravely?
2.  Is my creative faith turned on and tuned to the leading of the Holy Spirit in my witnessing?

3. Am I willing to be emotionally honest with the people to whom I witness?
4. How can I grow spiritually to become a more effective Christian by applying Toffler's survival kit concept?

# Three

# Interpersonal Motivation

When a person to whom you witness decides to commit his life to Christ and his church, he does so for reasons which are important to him. These reasons may not seem valid to his family, his friends, or even to the loving friend who leads him to Christ; but they are *crucial* to him, and you can increase your assistance to the Holy Spirit when you understand this. Psychologists call the reasons people do things "motives." And your success in winning people, even while following the leading of the Holy Spirit, can be greatly improved by having a clear understanding of motivation.

*Circle of Motivation*

It is generally premature to ask someone to do something unless we first understand how he feels. Consider the example of my back-fence neighbor who is trying to get his ten-year-old son to go to his piano lessons on Saturday morning, despite the fact that he sees the other lads heading off to the park for a ball game. He hates his lessons, and I see him trudging off as slowly as he can Saturday after Saturday. Yet he goes, not because his parents hope he will become a concert pianist in twenty years, but because he will not get the money he needs for a new baseball glove if he refuses to take his piano lessons. He is doing what his parents want, but *for his own reasons*. Many years from now Tommy may indeed be a concert pianist who continues to practice on Saturday mornings. But he will still be practicing for his own reasons and not for his parents'!

The same principle holds true in inviting men and women to commit themselves to Christ. For years I knew a woman who nagged her husband to commit his life to the Lord and attend church services with her. I admired her concern for his spiritual welfare; but one day when I was calling on her, she let her real motivation show for a moment. As we were talking she said how envious she was of the other women when their husbands attended worship services with them. Her eyes shone and her face became animated as her nonverbal communication emphasized her totally inadequate reasons for wanting him to make such a commitment. Not until years later, at a time of great personal stress when his job was phased out by his company and the family was in great financial need, did he turn over the affairs of his life to Christ. But he never did so because his wife thought it would be nice to have him attend church with her. He made his commitment for his own reasons when he became aware of how much he needed God's guidance in his life.

When you have won a friend's trust, he or she may listen politely to you and then choose to accept or reject the gospel claim on his life for reasons which will surprise you.

You will be more effective when you forget *your* reasons why he should live a Christian life and get into his world to understand his needs as he sees them before making your specific suggestions. To be sure, you should plan your witnessing the way one pastor did as he preached his Christ-centered messages. His people said that you never knew where he was going to start preaching, but you always knew where he was going to end: at the love and sacrifice of Christ!

In its simplest form, motivation is a closed circle. It starts with a need which may be out in the open or hidden. It can be diagramed like this:

As I understand it, your task as a witness is to get into this cycle at some point and show your friend how he can satisfy his spiritual needs. Once this need is satisfied the cycle is complete, and he is no longer actively seeking a solution. Obviously, that is the time he is most likely to respond to the promptings of the Holy Spirit, and to you as well. Give him your best at that time.


*Spiritual Bankruptcy*

In my work in the churches, as well as in other organizations, I find that women and men who are living secular, totally temporal lives make two mistakes which keep them from finding lasting spiritual satisfaction. Unfortunately, both of the errors are based on psychological concepts which are inadequate views of human motivation, but which have been widely taught in Europe and America. The mistakes follow the pleasure/pain principle taught first by Sigmund Freud and perpetuated by B. F. Skinner and the power/prestige principle taught by Alfred Adler and refined by Eric Berne in transactional analysis. In other words, the mistaken concepts are:

*If it feels good, do it.*
*If it's to your advantage, control it.*

The trouble with following either the pleasure or the power principle through life is that both lead to physical and emotional satiation and dissatisfaction in a very short while. There is a limit to how much pleasure one can absorb or how much power one can employ before he becomes deeply bored with his life.

I find that unfortunate men and women who live satiated or spiritually bankrupt lives have four major symptoms which block their discovery of satisfaction. The symptoms are:

*Opportunism*
*Fatalism*
*Collectivism*
*Fanaticism*

People are living by *opportunism* when they try to get along with inadequate, short-term values. They fail to make the personal investment needed to live satisfying lives over the long run. And it is the long run that the church has consistently insisted is crucial.

Claudia Harris, a young art teacher in Cincinnati, complained of the pain that living opportunistically caused her. She said: "There has to be basically something wrong with my life. I just go through the motions of teaching during the week in the classroom, for I hate my job. I live for the weekends, but when they arrive, I collapse and don't do anything worthwhile, or prepare for any other kind of work."

Claudia had a near terminal case of the "blahs" before she was thirty, drifting through life, working at a task which gave her no satisfaction, rejecting the gospel call on her life, and having no plans to make things better for herself. The last I heard, she was drifting in and out of sexual affairs which were crippling her search for happiness even more.

*Fatalism* is the tendency to become despondent and to believe that life is beyond salvaging. It appears in the assumption that men and women are not worth God's love and compassion. Therefore, the idea of accepting Christ's love is rejected as just a comforting fable from a superstitious time. Since life cannot be changed, Christianity is thought to have no relevance in modern life. Charlie Chaplin captured this sense of futility in the movie *Modern Times*.

The little comic, who often portrayed a tragic figure, was trapped in a huge set of gear wheels in one scene. Quite dramatically, it showed that he was serving the machinery of affluence rather than it serving humankind. Many people live with this sense of futility, as if they were so many replaceable units on a production line, until they give up in despair. They feel so dominated by big labor, big government, big church, and big education that they fail to see what a self-transcending relationship with God can do for them.

*Collectivism* occurs when a person abdicates his personal responsibility for making supportive choices about life, others, and God. This is not the concept of living in Christian community and love. Rather, it is allowing others to lead one into doing things and holding attitudes that are destructive. "Everyone else is doing it" is the watchword used to excuse one's lack of concern instead of growing toward what one could become in Christ.

Psychologist Stanley Milgram found that more than 60 percent of adults taken at random from the street would give what they believe to be potentially deadly electrical shocks to a stranger when they were told they would not be held responsible. They did this despite the victims' (who were actually taking part in the experiment) pleadings to be unstrapped from the apparatus because they had a "bad heart condition." The men and women did this as an official-looking man in a white laboratory coat continued to assure them that *he* had assumed full responsibility for their actions.

*Fanaticism* is a willingness to take away the rights and choices of others because their freedom is a threat to one's own needs. This is the Gulag Archipelago mentality found in the Soviet Union, as well as in the dictatorships of the Right. When someone wants to be different from the group, the fanatics shout "off with his head," for he no longer *deserves* any rights.

Archie Bunker, in the television series "All in the Family," is an example of a man who is ready to lash out at anyone he does not understand. Poor Archie is clinging by his fingernails to a life he no longer understands, for he cannot cope with the changes which are taking place. He hates anyone who succeeds in coping better than he. He wants to control his destiny, but has been so badly crippled by his lack of spirituality and by forces he does not understand that he is frozen in the past and cannot mature as a person must. This kind of person is a tragic figure who needs our love and support as we try to help him grow, even though he *is* painful to be around.

As you work to lead others to Christ and to fellowship in the church, be alert to discover these symptoms. Try to help these people who have problems see how harmful the symptoms are to their spiritual well-being. Even when some people commit their lives to Christ, they continue to show the symptoms which keep them from maturing in grace, unfortunately.

The long-term Lutheran study entitled *A Study of Generations*, conducted by a group of denominational psychologists, showed that about two out of every five Lutherans are living a life which Lutheran theologians call "Law-Oriented" rather than "Gospel-Centered." In case after case, the researchers found the same symptoms I have listed above. They are seen in the lives of those people who are trying to earn their standing with God instead of committing their lives to Christ in love and trust.

I have little doubt that every denomination has this same problem, for many unfortunate men and women who have accepted Christ's acceptance continue to live immaturely, failing to nurture themselves on the meat of the gospel, as is required for growth in the Christian life. They have not found practical ways of sharing the deep and eternal love of Christ with the people around them. Christianity remains a life preserver or a social activity, rather than a new way of life and love. I certainly do not want to be critical and harsh, for I lived in that manner for too many years myself before I made a personal commitment to Christ which allowed me to mature.

### A Spiritual Hierarchy of Personality

Over the years I have found a pattern to human needs as I pastored and conducted psychotherapy. I found that each person must move upward in three distinct stages to meet the needs that God has given humans. When the stages are pictured they look somewhat like the pyramid developed by Abraham Maslow some decades ago. There is a great difference, however, since they embody scriptural concepts at each of the three levels.

On the first level, physical love (called *eros* in the New Testament) relates to sensual pleasure. *Phileo* refers to brotherly love on the emotional or psychological level. Finally, at the summit of what people should be, *agape* or spiritual love is found. This love is our expression of divine love in our relationships. We reach that level by becoming self-transcendent in Christ, rather than merely self-actualizing as Maslow taught from his nonreligious viewpoint. When the three dimensions of personality are put into a diagram, they look like this.

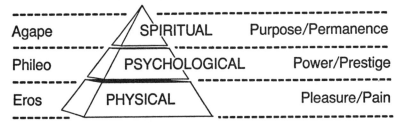

| Agape | SPIRITUAL | Purpose/Permanence |
| Phileo | PSYCHOLOGICAL | Power/Prestige |
| Eros | PHYSICAL | Pleasure/Pain |

When a person is living on the physical level, his needs for food, water, air, sex and shelter are predominant. They must be consistently satisfied before a person can seriously consider anything higher in the pyramid of motivation. This is equally true all through the stages of life. Man does not live by bread alone, except when he has no bread. Then that is often all he can think about. In his book *Baa Baa Black Sheep*, Gregory Boyington told of the days when he and other American fliers were captives of the Japanese. Since they were on a starvation diet, the men would dream of food for hours at a time. They would fantasize about the most outlandish recipes they could imagine, steal food from the guards, be beaten for their pains, and go back for more because this most basic of human needs was being denied. Only as a person is relatively satisfied at one level consistently can he give serious thought to the next level.

As an example, imagine a soldier in combat. He is living in physical danger, basically at the bottom tier of the diagram. He is deeply concerned about his need for safety, rest and food. Suppose, while crossing a river at night in a rubber raft, he falls into the water with his load of ammunition and weapons. As he sinks to the bottom, he struggles frantically in the murky darkness to get free from the weights that are going to take his life. He fights for life, wanting air more than anything else in the world. He does not think about his sweetheart back home, how well his comrades are doing, or whether he will be accepted into law school when he gets to the States. He is living with only one motivating factor, though it is very likely he will be praying as well as he knows how at the time.

When he finally struggles free of his weights and breaks the surface of the water, enemy bullets pepper the river around him. He gulps once or twice to fill his lungs and immediately dives back under the water he struggled, only a moment earlier, to get out of as soon as possible. Safety is still paramount to him. He reaches the bank, flops over it, and rejoins his friends who lead him to their bunker and relative safety. He rests a few hours, eats a warm meal, and only then draws a soggy picture of his sweetheart from his wallet. Then, because of his love and sexual needs he may write her a short letter.

Later in the day, he may volunteer once again to try to get across the river which nearly took his life. He does that because he now cares about the welfare of his friends who have been carrying on short-handed without him. In every war a large number of men will go absent without leave from their hospital beds, before their wounds are healed, to return to their comrades who are having to do double duty in their absence. They have no desire to return to danger, and they are not committed to the political reasons for the war. But they love their friends so dearly that they cannot remain safe while they are still in the struggle. *Phileo* love should not be minimized, for it is indeed a strong emotion which causes people to do noble things.

It may be years later before the young man, because of his need for permanence and purpose in his life, commits himself to Christ and matures to become a self-transcend- ing person who gives himself to humankind as he meets his highest order of needs.

In *Through the Valley of the Kwai*, Ernest Gordon told of his experiences in the jungles of Thailand when thousands of men in dire suffering committed their lives to Christ and took part in one of the modern miracles of grace. Gordon and virtually all of the men who had survived the very anteroom of hell there in the jungle committed their lives to humanitarian service in some manner. Gordon even- tually became dean of the cathedral at Princeton Univer- sity. They had grown in grace and never rescinded their commitment to Christ, who empowers us to mature to what we can become.

*Personality Patterns*

All people have the same basic needs in the physical, psychological and spiritual areas; but not all men and women act in the same way. The reason for this seeming paradox is that each person has inherited certain tendencies and learned unique ways of dealing with life and the people around him. Early in childhood each person discovers that certain attitudes and acts work better for him as he tries to meet his needs and to cope with life.

In those early years some youngsters learn to be little song and dance men who entertain others to get along. Other children become deputy commanders who tell others what the parents want done, as a means of feeling comfortable about themselves. Still other children try hard to understand everything they can about situations which affect them so they will not make any mistakes. Finally, some children work very hard to cooperate with the important adults in their little world, as a means of being at ease with them.

As we grow up, we reinforce these patterns and use them again and again because they worked well for us in the years we were discovering who we were and what we could do. Unfortunately, some people never seem to learn that another person's way of dealing with others is just as valid as their own. When this occurs, a man or woman may go through life relating only to those who allow him to remain comfortable, without any thought about what is happening. If we continue to use only the same approaches from childhood, without realizing that they were not ordained by God for all of humanity, we limit our effectiveness in relating well enough to become friends who can witness and have our friends listen seriously to us.

I called these consistent ways through which we unconsciously try to meet our needs *personality patterns* in my books *Nice Guys Finish First* and *Lovers for Life*. We normally interact with other people from a personal comfort zone which is designed to let us feel at ease most of the time. We all do this, and there is nothing wrong with it.

For example, if former president Gerald Ford had to stand up like a comedian to tell jokes to thousands of people, he would soon be distinctly uncomfortable. He would have been forced from his comfort zone. On the other hand, the late Senator Hubert Humphrey would have loved being in that situation. He was often more comfortable in the company of a large group of people, telling jokes and stories, than he was when alone. Forcing him to be quiet would push him from his comfort zone as quickly as forcing President Ford to act as a comic would for him. Learning how to identify personality patterns in others and how to predict what other people will do because you recognize their patterns will make it easier for you to relate supportively with others. It will also help you recognize their perceived needs, which is the second step in leading them to Christ.

In my previous books I discussed the large body of solid psychological research upon which the concept of four major personality patterns is based. I'll not go into it in this short book, but when the research was plotted on a chart, it looked like the diagram on p. 54.

Self-controlled people appear to be detached emotionally from others in their relationships, cool, and quite task-oriented. Self-expressive people appear to be close to those around them, warm, and very much people-oriented. Competitive people appear to be bold, fast-moving, and

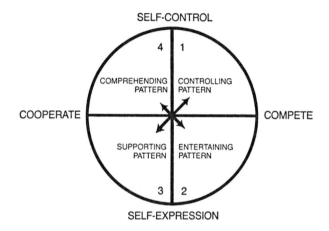

ready to dominate interpersonal situations. Cooperative people appear to be modest, slow-moving, and unwilling to dominate others. I have used the word *appear* several times, for the personality pattern diagram refers only to outward behavior. It has nothing to do with commitment, love, ambition, or loyalty. It is just the result in adulthood of what we learned was best for us in the years we were growing up. There is no good or bad place to be, unless one has become so extreme that he cannot accept the rights of others to act comfortably around him.

People who combine the traits of competitiveness and self-control fit into sector 1 on the chart. They are said to have the controlling personality pattern. Men and women who combine competitiveness and self-expression have the entertaining pattern as shown in sector 2. Those who combine cooperation and self-expression fit in sector 3, and have the supporting personality pattern. In the fourth sector are those who combine cooperation and self-control. They have the comprehending pattern.

Controllers can usually be identified by their fast-paced work habits, their self-control and their willingness to tell others what to do. They have the most trouble getting along with supporters because they have the most different traits in comparison to each other. Supporters tend to be kindly, willing to listen to people and not so task-oriented as controllers. Unfortunately, conflict can arise between them when the controller perceives the supporter as lazy. For at the same time the supporter may see the controller as manipulative and unconcerned with the finer things of life.

At the other diagonal of the chart are the entertainers, who are as fast-moving as the controllers but much more willing to tell others what they are feeling. They talk a great deal and are quick to relate to strangers. Their greatest interpersonal conflicts are with the comprehenders, who like to understand everything before they reach a decision. Because of these differences, an entertainer can think a comprehender cold and aloof, while he, in turn, can assume that entertainers are shallow blabbermouths.

A number of well-known people can be used as examples to help you understand the differences I am writing about in regard to personality patterns.

*Controllers:*    Richard Nixon, Billy Graham, John Wayne, Anita Bryant.

*Entertainers:*    Lyndon Johnson, Johnny Carson, Joan Rivers, Hubert Humphrey.

*Supporters:*    Dwight Eisenhower, Bob Schuller, Dinah Shore, Ed McMahon.

*Comprehenders:*    Calvin Coolidge, George McGovern, Katherine Hepburn, Tom Landry.

Here are some things to remember when you deal with

people from the different patterns. First, compare someone with the list above and decide which of the four categories he reminds you of. When you have identified his pattern, relate to him in a manner he will be comfortable with. After rapport has been established, you will probably slip back into your habitual pattern. A person can usually shift his pattern somewhat, so long as he thinks about what he is doing. Generally, when he gets down to the business at hand, he will revert to his normal manner of interacting. By then it will usually be all right; for he has started becoming a friend whose pattern, though different, is safe and acceptable.

No pattern is any better than any other, though people whose pattern is very strong frequently think that their own is best. When it comes to witnessing, some people fall into the error of testifying only to those whose patterns are like their own, for they are most comfortable with them. This limits anyone in relationships, for three-fourths of the people one meets operate in a different pattern. And if you are determined not to shift in order to help people relate better to you, you are limiting your effectiveness as a witness.

I am not asking you to change your personality pattern when you are witnessing, for that would smack of hypocrisy and emotional dishonesty. What I have done is give you a model for understanding people a little better and predicting with some realistic hope of success how they will act. By using this knowledge you can make it a little easier for people to trust you. I see this as a practical example of St. Paul's injunction for Christians to become all things to all men, as a means of increasing their effectiveness.

This isn't hypocrisy, but a practical manifestation of one's self-transcending love, for one of the key discoveries of the scientists conducting this research is not that our styles are different, but rather our willingness to adapt in expressing our concern and love for others.

*Personality Pattern Suggestions*

For controllers, be prompt, talk seriously about your reason for visiting with them, and do not spend too much time relating with small talk, for they don't usually need it. For entertainers, support their dreams and plans for the future, be entertaining and interesting to be with. Let them talk a lot and remain a good listener until it is your time to speak. For supporters, spend time relating warmly in a kind manner, for this is important to them. They will want to feel that you are concerned with the human aspects of the gospel. For comprehenders, logic and principles are the most important things, since they want certainty more than anything else in life. They don't care as much about relating as entertainers or supporters do, but they do like things to be neat.

In witnessing, controllers need to slow down and stop competing and telling so much. They need to offer warmth to those people on the bottom of the pattern chart. Entertainers need to slow down in expressing their ideas and feelings, as well as checking from time to time to see that others are still following them. Comprehenders need to talk with more enthusiasm and to accept the uncertainties of life, while telling others more of what they want for themselves. Supporters need to speed up and to make positive statements without hedging so much, to use tough love when needed, and to be authentic.

Adjusting your pattern in a new relationship will allow other people to become comfortable with you quickly, develop rapport, and help your testimony get off to a good start. It will allow you to reach a position where you can recommend a solution to the problems you recognize fairly quickly, because you have allowed your friend to remain in his comfort zone rather than making him defensive.

KEY CONCEPTS FROM CHAPTER THREE

1. People cooperate with us for their reasons and not ours.
2. According to the more perceptive psychologists, human needs include the physical, psychological, and spiritual.
3. There are four major personality patterns: the controllers, entertainers, supporters, and comprehenders.

KEY QUESTIONS TO ASK YOURSELF

1. Have I tried to understand my friend's motivation?
2. Do I understand his personality pattern as the way he tries to remain in his comfort zone?
3. Have I avoided the trap of liking only those people whose patterns allow me to remain in my comfort zone?

# ─────────Four─────────

# Interpersonal Relationships

Love is the key aspect of the positive relationship which allows you to witness effectively. As I understand love, it is not the sentimental emotion so often found in the movies and novels of our day. It is much more solid than that, for it is similar to the emotions that Jesus revealed all through his ministry. It includes the elements of *eros, phileo,* and *agape.*

At times, love can be totally accepting of others when they are vulnerable and in pain from the pressures of life. At other times it can include a fair degree of toughness which is based on our high expectations of another person who is struggling to become what he can be, but is fearful of committing his all to the outcome. At such a time you can remain accepting of the person but demanding of his best for himself, rather than for you. And, of course, your love should include a strong element of *agape,* which is divine in origin, because of your personal relationship with God.

When a person feels no love for another human, the emotion he does feel is not hate, as some suppose, but rather indifference. In Jesus' parable of the Good Samaritan, those who passed by the robbed and wounded man did not hate him. They were simply indifferent to his plight. Similarly, in our relationships with others, our true feelings about them are more frequently indifference instead of dislike. Because of each person's ability to interpret nonverbal messages without words being spoken, the attitudes we hold about others are understood and interpreted as a means of self-protection, so they rarely go unnoticed.

*Communicating Indifference*

Regardless of what we think we are communicating, other people interpret our concerns and actions through *their own* self-protective perceptions. The transactional analysis writers speak about people "devaluing" those with whom they associate in subtle ways. For example, I can remember sitting in an inquiry area following one of the early Billy Graham meetings in the Rose Bowl when I was attending Pasadena College. A young woman had come to speak with a counselor about committing her life to Christ. I soon noticed, however, that the counselor was making a crucial mistake that upset the seeker greatly.

While the counselor was speaking, she looked intently at the younger woman and leaned forward. But when the girl started to talk about her needs, the witness would turn away and tap her foot impatiently. It happened several times, and regardless of what she was *telling* the young woman, her most visible communication devalued and insulted her. It was so strong that I felt it some distance away. She was really saying, "I'm just waiting for you to shut up so I can take over again and set you straight."

About the third or fourth time it happened, the seeker stood up and walked away, completely frustrated by the nonverbal insults she was receiving. I suppose that the counselor was acting out of ignorance, or perhaps had some problem from home or work dominating her thoughts at the time, but everyone would have been better off had she quietly excused herself and asked another counselor to help the young seeker. She could do little good as long as she was preoccupied or impatient, regardless of how much she wanted to help.

Indifference may not always be as plain as a yawn; but if you do not make the effort to express your true concern for another person with deeds as well as words, it may be communicated quite forcefully. Because the first step in witnessing is relating warmly, you will have to listen attentively to what other people are saying with their verbal and nonverbal communication. Since no one wants to associate with someone who is indifferent, and since love is the opposite of indifference, you may have to work at learning how to express the love you have for your friend. Love has the major place in soul-winning, so much so that I have never known anyone to be led to a loving relationship with Christ without a personal relationship being established between the witness and the person to whom he is witnessing. For at the heart of successful soul-winning is the warm sharing of your Christian life and faith with another person.

Psychologists have discovered that techniques alone in psychotherapy are bound to fail unless they are applied with understanding and compassion. Each successful therapist has to be able to feel his client's needs as Sullivan did with the unfortunate patient at Wooster hospital. The old cliché, "I cannot hear what you are saying because what you *are* speaks so loudly," holds especially true in witnessing because we are dealing with the very core of a person's existence. Of course a happy balance has to be worked out, for good techniques without love will drive away the people we want to help, while love without methods will often be a hit-or-miss proposition.


*Expressing Love Effectively*

For some people, especially men in the American culture, the idea of dealing openly in love and affection causes concern. Many of us were reared with the notion that the John Wayne mystique of toughness and silence was the better way for a man to live. Of course, our male reluctance to express emotions may be one of the major causes of women outliving us by some eight years on the average; so the strong, silent myth has proven itself a real liability in more ways than one.

Fortunately, love is not some mysterious emotion that cannot be understood. It has three rather ordinary components which are:

*Understanding*
*Acceptance*
*Involvement*

Each of the three elements can be cultivated and expressed for the purpose of intensifying the loving relationship that is essential in leading a friend to Christ and to the fellowship of the church.

Develop your *understanding* of your friend by getting into his world and communicating on his channel. If he is interested in politics, sports, or history, learn about them so you can demonstrate how important they are to you also, *because he is important to you.* Don't be like the caricature of the street soul-winner who goes from stranger to stranger, grabbing them by the arm, asking, "Brother, are you saved?" insisting that you are not interested in anything but God. Everyone is interested in other things as they make a living, rear their children, care for their elderly parents, and experience many other aspects of living a full, rich life. And these are the handles by which you can grasp your friend's attention.

In his incredible fantasy novel, *Lord of the Rings*, J. R. R. Tolkien, who created a world based on Christian values and virtues, demonstrated how powerful an influence understanding has on our behavior. His character Gimli, the dwarf, had been insulted and humiliated upon entering the kingdom of Lothlorien. Blindfolded like a common thief, he had been brought before the king and queen of the elves. In his anger he stared moodily at the floor while Celeborn blamed the dwarfs for the problems they were facing. But when Gimli finally looked up to retort angrily, Queen Galadriel caught his eye. And where the dwarf expected to find condemnation and hate, he saw understanding and compassion. In that moment his anger faded to be replaced by love and he gave the queen his lifelong devotion.

I know no better way of demonstrating understanding than by allowing your friend to talk about something which is important and then paraphrasing his feelings in your own words. It works like this:

*Friend:* I spend so much time working and doing repairs on the house that I never seem to have time to spend with the kids.

*You:* Are you telling me that the routine things of life seem to keep you and the kids apart too much?

Or:

*Friend:* I would like to be a committed Christian, but we spend so much time at the cabin on the weekends that church is out of the question.

*You:* Do I understand you to be saying that recreation is more important to you than worship?

Paraphrasing a friend's statements is a powerful tool which both demonstrates your understanding without a doubt and also causes him to sort out his feelings about the things being discussed. In the second example above, he may have never really stopped to realize that he is actually putting recreation above worship. Besides, so few people ever use the technique that it is a potent instrument. We will consider it in more detail in a later chapter.

When you are *accepting* your friend regardless of his life style, sins, or shortcomings, you are simply following Jesus as he mingled with the people he was interested in helping. He certainly did not approve of the prostitute's self-crippling abuse of her God-given sexuality, the tax collector's greed and the many shortcomings he saw in the masses of his day. But he was able to differentiate between accepting the person and condoning his behavior. Psychotherapists have to do this with virtually every client. It is a narrow ledge upon which to walk, for simply accepting someone as he is may help condemn him to his present state of mediocrity. In our acceptance as a part of love, we have to go beyond that, as Jesus did, to accept people *for what they can become by God's strength.*

When you demonstrate verbally and nonverbally that *your* defenses are down in acceptance, that you refuse to live with the prejudices and pettiness that cripple the lives of so many Law-oriented church members, and that Christ is indeed the theme of your life, you are permitting your friend to lower *his* defenses. He senses that he can be honest with you without getting blasted with a self-righteous attack on his less-than-ethical behavior. You are pulling him into your net of acceptance, and people do respond to us as we first treat them.

Lowering your own defenses in acceptance will make it possible for someone to hurt you occasionally, but if you are to be understanding and accepting as a witness, that is a price you will have to pay from time to time. Any man or woman who lives in a pain-proof bomb shelter cannot be hurt, but that also blocks the sharing of love. Love does include a great deal of emotional vulnerability, but that cannot be avoided without becoming so hardened that love is gone.

My father is a man of great love and compassion who was always bringing in strays during the years of the Great Depression. He brought them home for food, clean clothes and a place to sleep. Most important of all, he gave them time to think without being under so much pressure to survive that they made serious mistakes. From time to time one of his wanderers took advantage of him, but he held fast to his principles of helping people. Incidentally, he taught me a lesson I have never forgotten. He said, following a theft of some small items, "I'd rather be robbed every second Thursday for the rest of my life than become so cautious that I couldn't ever be robbed again."

Demonstrate your acceptance by allowing others to be comfortable around you because you refrain from judgment. I feel it to be foolhardy for a Christian to judge anyone else, since we have neither the wit nor the maturity to care adequately for anyone but ourselves. The Scriptures make it quite clear that God reserves the responsibility of judging for himself and does not share it with us. Keep in mind that God promises to use the same yardstick on us that we use in judging others! Obviously, I don't know any more about God's judgment than is taught in the Scriptures, but as a psychologist I have learned that something Jesus taught about relationships is being accepted throughout the psychological professions today. In the

Sermon on the Mount Jesus said, "You can expect the way you treat people is the way you will be treated in return" (DeVille's Loose Translation). Psychologists are now calling this the Law of Psychological Reciprocity. For almost two thousand years most Christians assumed that the Golden Rule of Jesus was just a nice platitude which had no value in the "real" world. Now we understand that Jesus was teaching a basic law of interpersonal behavior that can be harnessed to make life more satisfying, as well as to improve our skills in soul-winning.

I have found a simple way to test the effectiveness of this law for yourself. Take the DeVille Sidewalk Test as you walk down a crowded sidewalk in your city. Smile at each person you meet. The vast majority will smile in return, nod pleasantly or even toss you a cheery greeting. On the next block frown at the people you meet, but be prepared to get out of the way! Many people will glare in return, slip between parked cars to get away from you, or stand with clenched fists until you are safely by. Just as Jesus taught, each person takes his cues about how to behave from the people he meets.

The same kind of response takes place in a witnessing relationship. If you act as an avenging angel of the Lord, people are going to be so busy protecting themselves from you that the friendship you need to influence them will never grow. On the other hand, if you send out the message that making a commitment to Christ is not very important, they will receive that message and probably shrug it off without considering the real consequences of such a rejection. Admittedly, you are taking an emotional risk when you become a friend of the people to whom you testify. You become vulnerable and can be hurt; but I do believe that God rewards us for our efforts, and the joy that follows winning others makes it all worthwhile.

In your witnessing find creative ways to become *involved* with your friend as supportively as you can. This third aspect of love is crucial, as I discovered in my youth. One of the greatest influences of my childhood was a pastor, a young man who was just out of school. He was especially effective at getting into the personal worlds of other people by becoming involved with them. His ministry was to the French fisherfolk of Louisiana. And while he frequently spoke against the evil of working on the Lord's day, I noticed that when the men were shorthanded he would go along to help with their nets, sometimes on Sunday afternoon.

One by one, those fishermen became staunch Christians in our church, and they stopped working on Sunday, also. He became involved with others, and they responded according to the Law of Reciprocity. We need to find ways of doing the same when expressing this final aspect of love.

## Avoiding Egocentric Predicaments

One problem that causes many people to fail in their witnessing is that of slipping into a self-centered predicament which keeps them from thinking clearly. This focusing all of one's attention on the problem takes place when we are worrying so much about our image or safety that we stop thinking. By focusing too rigidly on one aspect of a problem, we cannot relax enough to think clearly about alternative solutions.

Not long ago my oldest son received a call that his dog had been hit by a car and taken to a nearby animal hospital. Since he loves her, he immediately dropped everything he was doing and wheeled his motorcycle from the garage to go see how she was making out in surgery. He got on the bike and hit the starter button, but the engine wouldn't start. He tried again and again, until the battery ran down. Then, he used the kick starter over and over with no success. Finally, in response to his calls for help in pushing the bike, I went to the street. Since I was not nearly as concerned about his pet as he, I wondered aloud whether he had turned on the gasoline valve. As I mentioned that, a puzzled look came to my son's face, and he felt under the tank. The valve was closed, of course. He turned it on, I pushed him about ten feet, and the engine started!

He had been in an egocentric predicament which kept him from thinking as well as he normally does. I have no doubt that every reader of this book could think of a similar situation where he or she has focused so intently on something that everything else faded into insignificance. In witnessing, we can fall into this trap by worrying too much about our own egos, our own feelings in the situation. What we need to do when this is a possibility is to focus our feelings on *what* we are doing and *why* we are doing it. The easiest way to get out of such a predicament is to shift your feelings from yourself to your friend. If you have established a good relationship with him, he will not want to cause you any more pain or embarrassment than you want to cause him. Even if he feels no need to make a commitment of himself to Christ, he understands from your verbal and nonverbal communication that you are acting out of love. And if he is a normal person, he will respond according to the Law of Reciprocity.

If, while witnessing, you feel yourself becoming too concerned with your own fears, anxieties or needs, shift your feelings by projecting them toward your friend. Remind yourself *why* you are testifying to him. Ask yourself about the nature of your motives. Are they not to lead him to Christ, rather than to feed your ego at his expense? Is there anything in what you are asking him to do that is not for his benefit?

You will find, when you approach a possible egocentric predicament in this manner, the tension which blocks your effectiveness vanishes in a surge of love and concern for your friend. With increasing confidence you will be able to lead others to Christ with poise and effectiveness, for you have put the true reason for your testimony into its proper perspective. You may even find it helpful to put the above questions in a two- or three-step form to ask yourself about your motives before you visit with your friend.

## Going the Second Mile

Successful soul-winning requires that two distinct factors be woven together in your supportive relationship with your friend. These are the normal factors of *self-interest*, which we all have, and our God-given ability to become *self-transcendent*. A basic human trait is to ask, "What's in this for me?" And while this makes it possible to survive in a sometimes fiercely competitive world, too much emphasis on the self leads to all kinds of sin. When this happens, we selfishly lose sight of the fact that all men and women have to invest part of their lives in causes that are greater than themselves, especially while meeting their psychological and spiritual needs at the two highest levels of the pyramid. But there is nothing wrong with feeling good about yourself, because you are rising above your self-centered interests to offer your support and love to help a friend align his life with God.

Remain authentic enough to realize that you and any friend to whom you testify are going to have self-interest and self-transcending needs in the relationship. You both have normal characteristics which govern self-interest and other-interest. But when these are woven together into a mutually rewarding relationship for both of you, the chances are that you will be successful as you testify repeatedly to influence his decision.

If you are in a situation where the newness of the relationship still troubles you, and yet you feel led by the Holy Spirit to lead your friend to the Lord, remember that you are not working alone. You are doing God's work, and the Spirit is your partner as you discover his needs and make acceptable recommendations. Because you love your friend and you know that you are working with the Holy Spirit, be committed to God's work like the old-time Calvinists, about whom one man said, "I'd rather face a regiment of infantry than one Calvinist who was convinced that he was doing what God commanded." Trust God to do his part of the job, but be as prepared as is humanly possible. Strange though it seems, I have found that in all aspects of the Christian life, God seems to work best through well-prepared, hard-working men and women, like the Calvinists who shaped history!

Key Concepts from Chapter Four

1. Love consists of understanding, acceptance and involvement.
2. Wanting too much interpersonal security will weaken your resolve to give of yourself in love.
3. An egocentric predicament can be ended by focusing your attention on the needs of your friend and away from yourself.
4. Both self-interest and self-transcendent traits must be woven together in a mutually satisfying relationship.

KEY QUESTIONS TO ASK YOURSELF

1. Am I using the Law of Psychological Reciprocity by treating people the way I want them to treat me?
2. Am I being authentic, identifying personality patterns, and remaining out of egocentric predicaments by putting myself in my friend's place?
3. Have I made an effort to get into my friend's world so that he will see his need for Christ?

# Five

# Understanding Resistance

I have often heard it said that in business and politics knowledge is power. Certainly knowledge is also needed if you are to become an effective soul-winner. One very perceptive psychological writer, Hugh Russell, decided from his own observation and research that people most often do what we ask of them because they feel we understand them. If he is correct, knowledge about your friend is the key to successful persuasion. It will certainly help you understand why he is fearful of, or resistant to, making a spiritual commitment which can only enhance his life.

As your relationship with your friend deepens, you may discover that he has been deeply hurt by someone who did not know how to witness supportively. If this has happened, you will likely have to deal with protective feelings and resentment. He is also likely to have some prejudices which still cling from old assumptions about the nature of a

Christian experience. I found this out when discussing spiritual needs with an aviation industry executive last year.

Paul and I had known each other for some years, often flying to the Experimental Aircraft Association convention together. From time to time I mentioned my personal intent to keep Christ at the center of my life, but he had not seemed interested. Not until a friend of ours crashed and burned on a seemingly routine flight did he ever bring up the subject of his spiritual health. In fact, as he started asking questions, I sensed a deep longing there for the purpose and permanence which only God can give to a person. It took only a few minutes for him to abandon his seeming disinterest and commit himself to Christ. Later, he wrote to me about it:

> For years I had a misconception of what a personal commitment of my life to Christ was all about. I had some way-out notions about never doing anything again but attending prayer meetings and revival services. But most of all, I suppose, I resented the way you talked so casually about knowing God. I felt as if you were claiming to have God in your pocket. Now I do just what you did. I *know* the God you've spoken so personally about. And while I don't claim to have him under my control, I do understand your faith. I have a sense of his care, his love, and his presence in my life. I don't really understand why my old assumptions were so wrong. As I look at what has happened, I can see that you were simply telling it like it is.

While moving through feelings of resistance or resentment, you must develop a supportive climate in which you both feel free to discuss the more serious aspects of your lives. Fortunately, there are a number of methods you can use to neutralize defenses, methods which will not have bad aftereffects if you are using them with love and concern for your friend.

*Neutralizing Defenses*

There is probably no better way to reduce initial tension than asking someone to tell you something about himself that you sincerely want to know. There are few better icebreakers in a stalled relationship than saying something like:

"I would like to understand your feelings about this a little better."

"Tell me what you mean by that statement. It really makes sense."

"It seems that you've been very successful all your life. How do you make things work so well for you?"

Remember that words convey only 7 percent of any conversation, however; so you must remain authentic as you ask for more information from him. If you are nervously looking at your watch as he talks, he'll sense the difference in the messages and decide that you are not really as interested as you say. If you do not want to hear about his life and needs, don't say that you do; or he will certainly be confused by the difference in the messages you are conveying. But do not try to testify to him either; you will only make it more difficult for a more compassionate person to lead him to Christ later in his life. I personally feel there are few more serious mistakes made in witnessing than memorizing a canned presentation that is delivered in the same way, regardless of the circumstances or personality patterns involved.

Another way to get through a person's defenses is to offer him a sincere compliment. Be careful about doing this, however, since all salesmen are trained to do the same thing almost automatically. Unless you remain authentic, with your words and tone conveying the same message, you could give the impression that you are being manipulative when you do not intend to be. The effective use of interpersonal relationships is no more manipulative in itself than is the use of music by a church choir to set a worshipful mood on Sunday morning, or the use of good speaking skills by a pastor to persuade people to make a personal commitment to Christ.

I have never found a person who could not sincerely be offered a compliment. However, it should be done carefully to avoid stirring up emotions which have nothing to do with the commitment of his life to Christ. For example, if you point to a picture in someone's office and say, "That's a beautiful scene," you may discover later that he keeps it only because his mother-in-law painted it. He detests the thing and shows it only to keep peace with his wife! You could have said, "That's an interesting scene." Then he might have grunted noncommittally, and you could have interpreted his body language and let the whole thing drop. He may have even felt secure enough with you to tell you that he dislikes it but prefers peace to discord. Then your understanding of him would have been increased, without creating a needless issue between you.

If your friend has trouble talking about himself, you can help him get started with a statement that will grasp his attention. You might say, as a means of bringing things into focus:

"What would it mean in your life if you could find a solution to the most serious problems you have?"

"I've come to offer you the greatest help I know how to give a friend."

"I've stopped in today because our friend Alice Kent suggested I do so."

*Asking Questions*

Any of a hundred different opening statements may be used if they are authentically fitted to your friend's situation. Such statements can get him talking about himself, his family, his work, or his needs. As he talks you are better able to enter into the discovery part of witnessing as you recognize the areas of his life with which he is unhappy. When I've reached this point, I simply ask him if it would be all right for me to ask him a few questions.

The majority of people with whom you have related well will give you permission immediately. A few comprehenders, however, may want to know why you are asking them questions. In that case, as in the rest of witnessing, honesty is the best policy. Tell them that you want to understand them better and that questions will help you do so.

Asking permission to question a friend is important for two reasons. First of all, it enables you to find the information you need without sounding like an inquisitor or a busybody. In the second place, it will allow you to guide the conversation toward spiritual issues rather than allowing it to ramble along pointlessly from one issue to another.

There are two different kinds of questions to be used: *fact-oriented* questions and *feeling-oriented* questions. Fact-oriented questions relate to a person's family background, kind of work, areas of interest, and so forth. Such questions will let him relax with ideas which are nonthreatening and easy to answer. They also demonstrate that you are concerned with his entire life and not just recruiting members for your church (as he may see it at this point). Finally, they will supply you with important information needed to demonstrate your understanding and guide your testimony into areas which are most likely being touched by the Holy Spirit. Examples of fact-oriented questions are:

"Where do your children go to church/school?"

"How long have you been working here in the city?"

"How old are your children now?"

Feeling-oriented questions are more personal and often more difficult to answer. These relate to a person's beliefs, childhood experiences, views of God, present religious practices, and philosophy of life. As you ask feeling-oriented questions, phrase them so he cannot answer them with a simple "yes" or "no" answer. It will do little good to ask a question like, "Do you think everyone should be a Christian?" He will probably tell you that they should, and you are back where you started with him seated silently awaiting your next silly question.

You can stimulate his thinking about spiritual things better with an open-ended statement like: "Some people find that making a commitment to Christ is a simple step of faith, while others have to agonize over the decision for a long time. Why do you suppose people have such differences?" Other examples of feeling-related questions are:

"Can you tell me why you and Carla stopped attending church when you arrived here in the city?"

"What did your parents teach you about the relationship a person should have with Christ?"

"What kind of value system are you and Ben bringing into your home as you establish a family?"

As you try to discover how your friend perceives his needs, remember that he will typically respond much more positively if he realizes that you really understand him and his feelings. It is more important, by far, to demonstrate your understanding from time to time than to impress him with your brilliance or overwhelm him with Scriptures while daring him to refute you. In either case you have already lost the battle for your friend's commitment. You *really* need to understand his needs, attitudes and fears before you can wisely recommend a solution to his life's problems. Continue to show your understanding by paraphrasing his key statements from time to time.

If he has been critical of the church, you can say something like this:

"Let me see if I understand what you are telling me about the church. You say that at times you find a gap between what people profess and what they actually do. Is that the way you feel about it?"

Of course it's the way he feels about it, for you are simply repeating his statement in your own words. Because people ordinarily never do this, it will demonstrate a depth of understanding he has rarely seen before; and it will open doors for you to continue deeper and deeper into his self-system and finally recommend a personal commitment in a way which is shaped to help him the most.

Be alert for the creation of tension, however; his increasing awareness of what he should do compared to what he has done may produce deep feelings of one kind or another. Typically, people handle tension by solving the tension-creating problem *or* by getting rid of the tension-producing element—you!

When you sense the tension becoming too great to handle and you see nonverbal signs that he is going to end it in the second way, relieve his stress by relating a quote or telling a third-person story which makes your point indirectly. You can say something like:

"Harry, some of our friends tell me that in thinking about their spiritual growth and committing their lives to Christ, certain things bother them more than others. Can you think of anything that might bother you?"

Not only have you shifted the emphasis, you have also

given him permission to discuss any fears or prejudices he may have without damaging the relationship with you. He can talk freely without feeling guilty about it then or later.

Giving a person authentic permission to disagree openly is something few men and women ever do, for most people are more interested in winning arguments than in winning souls. Your unusual act will allow him to bring his own feelings and thoughts out in the open, examine them without being threatened, and, following the Law of Reciprocity, be willing to listen to your testimony when you share it with him and ask for a commitment.

There is also an element of catharsis, or freeing-up, which occurs when one discusses things that have long been hidden. One gains a certain amount of relief from discussing his feelings openly and is less likely to slip into an egocentric predicament than he would with his feelings bottled up inside because he is too polite or fearful to discuss them.

Since so many people in our society are taught to talk about facts rather than feelings, your attempt to understand someone will often open a floodgate of emotions that may amaze you at times. So few people understand the power of being accepting that most people really open up to someone who is willing to deemphasize his own needs in their favor.

I can remember the first time I really used this approach with a stranger. I was on a train with a businessman from Chicago when I decided to really try to understand him rather than telling him about myself. In a short time he sensed my willingness to listen, was reassured by my nonthreatening statements, and began pouring out his feelings. For a solid hour he told me about the frustrations of his life: the problems he and his wife were having, his teenage daughter's rebellious moods, the uncooperative bankers he was dealing with, and even his lazy supervisors at the plant. By the time he got off the train the extent of his relief was quite evident in his nonverbal communication. Because I had set the stage for him to express the problems that were close to him, he bounced off the train a different man from the one who boarded.

When you allow a friend to rid himself of unproductive tension or concepts, your permission for him to do so may be verbal or nonverbal. You can say:

"I see . . ."

"Tell me more about that."

"I understand what you're saying."

"Go on."

"I'm with you."

Nonverbal communication is every bit as effective. You can:

Lean forward in your seat

Nod wisely

Open your arms

Change your facial expression

Shift the tone of your voice

Pat him on the arm

Always phrase your questions in nonthreatening terms and listen sincerely to help relieve fears and anxieties which frequently block him from making a positive decision for Christ.

*Five Serving Men*

Rudyard Kipling, whose poems are still read by millions of people, wrote that each writer has five serving men to help him get his message across. The words, used in context, are:

*What* happened to catch your interest?

*Where* did it happen?

*When* did it take place?
*Why* did it happen?
*Who* was involved?

The use of these five words, at least mentally as you strive for better understanding, will allow you to get more quickly into your friend's world and discover his needs.

Finally, to get him talking and to reveal more feelings so you can present the gospel choice in the best light, turn his imagination on with "suppose" questions. You might ask him something like the following:

"Suppose your life goes on like it is now. What will be the outcome before the kids are grown?"

"Suppose you and Larry continue quarreling so much. How long will your home be secure?"

"Suppose the Scriptures are right, and Christ is the only way acceptable to God. What would happen if you failed to commit your life to Christ?"

"Suppose your children grow up with strong spiritual values. What will probably happen to them in this age of confusion and change?"

Once more you are doing something that few other people ever do, and you will probably have his total attention. Your statement and then a "suppose" question become a blackboard on which he can write his own answer better than you ever could.

Key Concepts from Chapter Five

1. People do what we ask because they feel we understand them, rather than because they understand us.
2. Getting a person to talk about his life, love and labor is a great way to rid a relationship of tension.
3. Your questions should first be fact-oriented.and then feeling-oriented as you search for needs to meet.

4. "Suppose" questions are free-form imagination triggers which are very valuable in your testimony.

KEY QUESTIONS TO ASK YOURSELF

1. Am I asking fact- and feeling-oriented questions to discover how my friend feels about his need for Christ?
2. Am I using Kipling's five serving men: what, where, when, why, and who?
3. Am I setting his imagination free with "suppose" questions as a means of getting him to think about the new concepts I am discussing?

# ─── Six ───

# Listening with the Heart

It is an unfortunate thing that so few people really learn to become good listeners. This weakness begins in childhood when we are taught to speak out and to do things, rather than to put ourselves in the place of others in order to better understand them. Even the comprehender who asks what people are doing is usually communicating from a self-centered position, instead of trying to discover what other people really feel.

This common inability to listen complicates a person's testimony in several ways, for it keeps him from discovering what is actually going on in the mind of the other person. When a witness pauses long enough to find that out, he will have a much better chance of persuading the other to commit his life and then improve its quality in the Lord. Often the people who listen the least while speaking about spiritual matters are the newly converted Christians who are so excited about the wonder of their relationship to Christ that they forget each person always makes up his own mind about such a choice.

Fortunately, most people will make an allowance for such persons; but it will surely help their testimony if they learn how to channel their enthusiasm and love constructively in their desire to help others. Learning how to listen with their eyes and bodies, as well as with their ears, will certainly help them become more effective as they share the gospel.

## Mistakes in Listening

It seems to me that Christians have a number of bad habits when they listen to others during a time of witnessing. Here is a list of some I have observed as I deal with people and teach my *Sharing the Faith* seminars.

*Prejudging people by assuming what their answers will be.* This is manifested by an impatience which does not allow the person time to think through his feelings and to answer for himself. The witness assumes he knows the answer and takes charge in advance, rather than taking time to discover what the real answer is.

*Spending too much time on facts and not enough on feelings.* People do this when they believe that decisions are clear-cut and logical, rather than based on emotions as most decisions are. Every decision that a person makes is related to his feelings in some way, regardless of how well that is concealed with logic and facts. This isn't wrong, as we frequently believe, but just the way humans behave. We want to be coolly logical, but we seldom are in crucial choices.

*Ignoring the real meaning of the words the other person uses.* This happens when we assume that his world is the same as ours. Actually, every person has experienced a reality which is somewhat different from anyone else's, and that should be considered when trying to understand him. Try to catch the nuances which he applies to the words in his conversation.

*Letting our feelings block our sensitivity to his needs.* In anything which is as personal as witnessing, it is easy to let your own ego get in the way. If you sense this happening, stop and look into your motives. Are you doing this for your good and not his? In that case, set your own ego on the shelf for a while and be as humble as Jesus was when he washed the disciples' feet.

*Permitting ourselves to be distracted by our own secular interests.* We all have to earn a living, rear our kids, and make mortgage payments, of course; but when witnessing, leave them behind. If something comes unbidden to mind, gently press it aside with an internal reminder that first things must come first. Do not berate yourself, but simply push it aside and return to the business at hand.

*Pretending to listen while planning to take charge as soon as he pauses for breath.* Not only does this devalue the other person, it confuses him, for you are sending out conflicting messages. You are saying that you want him to tell you about his needs, but your body language is telling him to shut up so you can take charge and tell him what you want him to do.

*Going off on tangents which do not lead him toward Christ.* This is a problem most often faced by people at the right of the personality pattern chart, for they tend to play mental leapfrog more than supporters and comprehenders do. When this happens, you must calmly turn your mind back to the central issue of the visit. As he or she becomes a good friend, you will have many things to talk about; but in witnessing, keep to the other person's need to commit his or her life to Christ.

*Three Aspects of Listening*

Listening is important for many reasons, but it is always crucial when establishing the key *interpersonal discovery* you and your friend need to make to lead him to a clearly understood, life-changing decision for Christ. An interpersonal discovery, such as a psychotherapist establishes with a client, is necessary before you can testify in a way that will assure his really hearing your recommendation and also recognizing the validity of it. Remember that a person will not normally accept your solution to a problem he has not yet perceived. By establishing an interpersonal discovery with him, he has become aware of his problem and will then be able to see the validity of your answer. I will return to that a little later, but I want you to realize that listening is the key to establishing the discovery.

When we are listening to another person, an attempt to understand him takes place on three levels. The first level is that of *selective listening*. By listening in this way we are sifting the speaker's words and feelings for those which are relevant to the situation. This allows us to pinpoint his problems *as he sees them* and to discover those emotions which are most likely to motivate him to respond to the Holy Spirit's wooing.

Not long ago I was talking to a man about his need for Christ. As I listened, I discovered a resistance to spiritual concepts which made me wonder if I could enter his world without establishing a long, supportive relationship. As I used nonverbal rewards such as an occasional nod, a quiet "I see," and other reinforcers to keep him talking, he said more than he had originally intended. He spoke about the problems he had in growing up. Because I was listening selectively, I caught a sense of longing for the mother who had died when he was only a child. It was a brief glimpse into his past as he quickly passed to another topic. I did not let it die, however, but returned to it with a few feeling-oriented questions in a low-key voice.

His answers revealed that his mother had, indeed, been a devout Christian woman who had taken both him and his sister to church and Sunday school every Sunday until her death. His father had remarried, and neither the man nor the stepmother was interested in the children's spiritual growth. After his mother's death, the children stopped attending church altogether. I let him tell me about this and caught an even greater sense of longing in his voice, so I said that many people tell me the early years of life leave an impression nothing can erase. Immediately tears came to his eyes and he said: "I haven't always lived as I should have, but that woman was a jewel. If there is a heaven my mother deserves to be there."

As he spoke so sincerely, it was obvious to me that his shell of self-protection had vanished in the deeply felt love for his mother. Without intruding into his memories, I told him about Raymond Moody's research into life after death and pointed out that his mother had been setting the stage for a spiritual life for the children when she had been stricken. I suggested that God had spared her long enough for her to teach both of the children the way they should live. I told him that I felt it would honor her and bring her teachings to maturity if he completed what she had obviously been working toward forty years earlier. In a few minutes he agreed, and we knelt beside his desk where he made a commitment of himself to Christ.

That decision has made a major impact on my friend's life as it should, of course. And that isn't all. That night he called his sister on the West Coast, and they spent several hours on the phone as he led her to Christ, also. My point is this, however. I could not have reached him so quickly had I not stopped talking long enough to *listen selectively* to what he was telling me. It was when I heard the longing in his voice that I recognized the direction the Spirit was leading me.

*Responsive listening* is as important as selective listening in guiding a person to a wise decision. Perhaps you do not realize how much a responsive listener can set the direction a conversation takes by simply reinforcing it from time to time. Every psychologist or psychiatrist uses this method with his clients all the time. The process is simple and in witnessing it works like this:

> *Respond to the concerns that are important to his decision to commit his life to Christ and remain uncommunicative about the things which are not.*

If you are witnessing and your friend starts talking about his vacation, listen selectively—but say nothing as he talks. Let him make his statement but remain motionless and don't say anything. If, however, he mentions that his family was in a dangerous storm on the lake and their lives were saved in a near miraculous manner, reinforce his speaking about that.

As I mentioned earlier, the rewards you give him for talking about spiritual matters may be verbal or nonverbal. If he tells you that he attended church in high school, a quiet "I see" or "That's interesting" will usually keep him talking about those things. So will a nod, a smile, a literal pat on the back, or any other show of approval. By responding to the things that are important in spiritual matters, after you have related warmly enough to gain rapport, you can shape the course of the conversation and help another person recognize the elements in his life which have been overlooked.

Many times in my counseling I have had people sent to

me by court action, people who came with a great deal of resentment and fear. They had no intention of telling me anything about their lives. Yet, in the vast majority of cases I was able to gain their trust and persuade them to talk freely about their problems in less than an hour by using the art of responsive listening.

The point to remember is this: Use your skills legitimately and for spiritual purposes as you respond to the things which are important, and do not react to those which will distract from your friend's discovering his need for Christ.

The third kind of listening is *heartfelt listening*. When you listen in this manner, you endeavor to share the hurt, the anxieties, the longings, and the joys of life as experienced by your friend. Not only can you feel them with him, you become skilled in expressing your understanding of them as well. I find it helpful to listen until he reaches a crucial statement and then use the paraphrasing technique. I may say: "Let me see if I understand what you're telling me. Are you saying that life has become very complex now that you're married and rearing a family of your own? Is that what you're telling me?"

A variation of that could be, "Do I understand you correctly that. . . ?" Or it could be, "Is what you are trying to tell me that you. . . ?" Or, "Do you mean you feel that. . . ?" At that point you should sum up the important facts and feelings he has been telling you, particularly as they relate to his need for Christ. It often goes like this:

"Let me see if I understand what you've been telling me. You and Harry are having too many quarrels, he shows too little interest in you, and the kids seem to be having more and more problems adjusting in school. Is that what you've said? And you feel that life is passing you by now? I can see why you would be depressed at times. I admit if I were in your place, with such things happening, that I'd often be discouraged, also. But tell me, do I understand you to be saying that you're looking for some way to get your life back on track? Is that what you're really saying as we talk?"

If your friend *agrees with your summation* of your heartfelt listening, you have reached an interpersonal discovery point in the conversation; and you are ready to ask for a commitment.

*The Interpersonal Discovery*

In this case, your friend has not yet committed her life to Christ; but you have now paid your dues to her because you have become involved, listened to her problems, demonstrated your understanding of her feelings, and reached an interpersonal discovery point that she has just accepted. In her mind you have earned the right to recommend a solution to her problems. She has not guaranteed that she will accept your solution, but she will most certainly listen to you.

Until you have earned the right to witness by relating warmly and recognizing her needs, in her mind you do not know enough to tell her how her life should be run. But if you have dissolved the interpersonal barriers with your love and acceptance, you have earned the right to witness, telling her what a commitment to Christ can do for her in her specific situation. Up to that point a Christian life style has probably remained a generality, but you have now made it a very personal thing. And she will most likely listen attentively and hope that you do have a solution for her problems. You have set the psychospiritual stage for success. With the help of the Holy Spirit, you have established a spiritual climate in which her decision is made reasonable and desirable.

Another interpersonal discovery can be stated this way: "I want to make sure I understand your feelings about this. Are you telling me that your family is having emotional problems because your company keeps moving you around the country faster than the kids can adapt, that you and Betty stay so tense you fight over meaningless things, and that life seems rootless and without purpose as you shift from place to place? Do I understand you to say that?"

If he agrees that you have correctly understood his situation and emotions, such a summation puts you in the position to become an advocate for Christ. Your friend knows that you understand him, that you accept his feelings, and that you are not judging him in some self-righteous psychological game. Because you have been listening in a way that few people do, following the Law of Reciprocity, he will most likely listen to you as you become Christ's advocate who recommends a solution tailored to meet his situation. This is when you recommend Christ as the answer to his problems. You are his loving, supportive friend who is deeply concerned about his well-being, and that means more than words can tell in his reaching a positive decision.

To keep from sounding like a snake oil salesman at a county fair, you must deal with your friend from one of the three basic areas (relating, recognizing and recommending) at all times. As you stay in these three crucial postures, you will discover that witnessing, like life, does not always move in a straight line. You'll be interrupted by telephone calls and have to fall back to discover more facts or feelings before recommending the solution. Children will come home hungry from school, and you will have to adjust once more, and so it goes. The positions will shift and fluctuate as you conduct your soul-winning interview, but you should always know which phase you are in with him and remain alert and aware of where you want to lead your friend. In this way you can remain consciously effective in soul-winning.

KEY CONCEPTS FROM CHAPTER SIX

1.  Listening must take place at three levels: selective, responsive and heartfelt.
2.  Bad listening habits include: prejudging others, ignoring feelings, ignoring word meanings, focusing on personal needs, becoming distracted, pretending to listen and following tangents.
3.  The intermediate goal is to reach an interpersonal discovery that sums up his perceived needs.

KEY QUESTIONS TO ASK YOURSELF

1.  Am I allowing my friend to express his authentic feelings?
2.  Am I reinforcing his focus on the key issues of life and faith?
3.  Am I putting his feelings into words as a means of understanding him and demonstrating my understanding?
4.  As a patient, consciously effective witness, do I aim for an interpersonal discovery before making a recommendation about Christ?

# Seven

# Presenting the Gospel Choice

After you have reached an interpersonal discovery point, you have earned the right to ask for a commitment and have also learned to phrase your invitation in terms that make sense to your friend. As you tailor your presentation for him, you must remain aware of the fact that he will still be asking himself some crucial questions. The way you handle these questions, even if he never puts them into words, may well determine the outcome of your testimony. Through the years I have heard many questions, but they most frequently include some variation of the following three.

*Three Crucial Questions*
*Will my commitment to Christ do for me what you say?*
When your friend asks himself this question, he is not necessarily doubting your sincerity so much as your judgment. Most people know how much the human mind

can deceive itself, and he may have been witnessed to in such glowing terms in the past by immature Christians that he puts your recommendation in the same category. When you see this doubt appearing, assure him that you do not see a Christian commitment as a magic, mystery cure, but rather an aligning of his priorities with those of God. Because of this, he will be able to live with joy and peace, despite the problems and pressures we all encounter in an affluent society. He can do this more effectively because certain aspects of his nature have been transformed in Christ.

*Is this the best solution for my life?*

Your friend may feel that he or she should not act in too hasty a manner, that life may offer him a better solution later if he keeps seeking. I find that most people do feel a resistance in making a decision at this point in my witnessing interview, whether it comes from ignorance, anxiety of the unknown, selfishness, or evil. Most people realize that making a commitment of their lives to any great cause includes demands made upon their time, talents and money, and this one is no different. Following Christ has no monetary cost, but along the way we are required to give of ourselves in love and service. To try to get by in the Christian life without helping others is to remain immature and selfish. Some writers call this cheap grace, for there is little spiritual value in it. If God has demands upon your life in service or sacrifice, he will grant the grace and blessings which go with the service. Be sure that your friend understands that.

*Will this decision help me for the rest of my life?*

Your friend may have known people who began the Christian life with the expectation that it would end all pain, problems and temptation, only to become dis-couraged and fall by the wayside, as Jesus observed in the parable of the sower. In any case, he will certainly have known people who professed Christianity while not living up to the standards and obligations God has set for us. He may also be wondering if he has the strength needed to meet the requirements of a committed life for as long as he lives. We know that he cannot, any more than we can in our own strength; for Christianity is far more than a moral value system, but he does not yet recognize the sustaining strength that God gives to the people who have committed their lives to him.

Look for the indications that your friend is asking himself these three general questions. Be prepared to deal with them in an emotionally honest manner, for little will be gained by keeping them hidden rather than dealing with them directly. Set the example for him to discuss whatever he wants to find answers to about his spiritual choice.

*The SAB Process*

As you answer your friend's questions, you can use a three-step technique to assure him that he is doing the right thing. This has been called the SAB method; for it contains the three elements that you need to make clear to him, namely, that receiving Christ and worshiping him offers a *solution*, an *advantage*, and a *benefit* which will last as long as he lives, and beyond.

The solution to his problem, which both of you now understand because it was spelled out in the interpersonal discovery, is to bring Christ into his life. This includes telling him what salvation is. You want him to realize what receiving Christ's acceptance actually means and what he should expect. Don't overwhelm him with facts or feelings but touch upon both.

The following comments are what a Christian woman

might say to another woman who perceives her need to bring an end to the destructive conflicts in her marriage:

"Jane, you've told me that you and John need to stop your continual bickering with each other. As I understand the problems you face in marriage, it seems to me that you need the grace of the Lord, the strength he gives to men and women to live successfully after they commit their lives to him. All through the Scriptures Jesus spoke of the way husbands and wives should treat one another in love and understanding. I believe that if you would commit your life to Christ, much of the conflict you and John have would vanish in the new spiritual love you would be able to express to him.

"I don't know about your marriage; but in my own, things were never one-sided. Gerry and I had our problems and still do at times, for neither of us has become an angel. But when I became a Christian in fact as well as in name, God showed me how I was causing many of our conflicts. When I committed my life to Christ, I was able to stop putting pressure on him; for I had this sense of completeness for the first time. And, you know, that allowed Gerry to change. He stopped being so defensive with me. I really believe that you need to receive Christ into your life as your personal Savior, commit your life to him, and let the Spirit start guiding your marriage."

The second step, the *advantage*, can often be shown in the most favorable light by telling a third-person story which makes your point. This shows that other people besides yourself have found satisfaction in the Lord. You might say something like this:

"You remember Alice Hanson from back home, don't you? Do you remember the boy she married from Porterville, Harry Downs? They had three kids right away and then started having the same kinds of problems we did.

They were separated like we were, three or four times, and nearly divorced. They would quarrel, feel hurt, and then reconcile. It was a real soap-opera life for more than ten years as they tried to work things out for themselves in their own strength. About a year ago Alice turned to Christ the way millions of people are now doing, including President Carter. She really committed her life to him. She felt renewed spiritually, but things didn't change with Harry immediately. So she started praying for him, for the children, and for the relationship. And because she was free enough to start maturing in Christ, she started taking part in the women's seminars at our church. She found that many of the things she was doing drove Harry right up the wall. The other women told how they had done the same things out of their own frustration, until they learned better ways of living with the people they love.

"So Alice started praying in another way. She stopped praying for a miracle which would turn Harry into a knight in shining armor and started praying that God would help her become a better woman, help her mature spiritually. *And he did!* She stopped nagging and criticizing Harry so much, and he couldn't help seeing the change in her. To make a long story short, he found her a lot more interesting and lovable than she was before, more like the girl he had fallen in love with before the pressures of life closed in on her. Her living witness to him led him to church for the first time in years, and he soon made his own decision for Christ. Then, their life together smoothed out. They study the Scriptures, read the kinds of books that help them grow, and have family prayers with their children. Best of all, they lovingly accept each other and themselves in God's love and mercy.

"I'm convinced that something that great could happen to you if you let the Lord have his way in your life. We're good enough friends for you to know that I wouldn't want to cause you any problems. And I know from my own life as well as from Alice's, that a commitment of your life to Christ can only help you, John, and the kids. And I can tell you several examples of how marriages have been saved in our church alone."

The third step in the process is showing the *benefit*, or how people will feel when they make the decision for Christ. It could be stated like this:

"Jane, there is nothing like a personal experience with Christ, anywhere. Being reborn in him is real and satisfying, for it gives you a deeper sense of happiness than anything else in life. You have told me how you and John love each other despite the quarrels you have. Having that love is great, but you need more than that. I found that confessing my shortcomings and sins and taking my burdens to God gives the lasting self-esteem, the peace, and the joy I needed for so long. I feel good now about my life and my worth. And I know you well enough to know that you will find it as satisfying as I have. The work I do in the church gives me a sense of fulfillment since there is a permanence there which is connected to God himself. For the first time in my life, I know that everything is all right and that I'm really contributing positively to the people I love.

"Now that I understand your problems better, I'm sure you would find a similar satisfaction for your life also. I see that you could have the kind of marriage and relationship Alice and Harry found after they committed their lives to Christ and became active in the church. Isn't that what you really want for yourself and your family? Don't you want the peace that comes from committing your life completely to Christ?"

Remember that the *solution* is accepting Christ as Savior,

while the *advantage* relates the way a personal relationship with God empowers a person to live above the banal, soap-opera lives that so many people endure. The *benefit* is the way a person feels about himself and others as a result of his choice. In advocating a personal commitment to Christ, keep the three separate; but let them work for you as a single process for helping other people understand the outcome of following your suggestion for renovating their lives through God's love and concern.

*What to Emphasize*

I find that few middle-class Americans I know respond initially to a strong condemnation of sin as a means of attracting them to Christ. Few people today, except for skid-row derelicts, people like my friend Kenny Jones, and emotionally disturbed men and women have a strong sense of sin, despite the way we humans have ravaged the earth, destroyed each other's cities, and misused our sexuality. Regardless of the reasons, I find people do respond better to my testimony that living in Christ does more to ease the pain of a frustrated life than anything else.

In some way, having a sense of sin has become a giant anachronism to a great number of men and women. I do not believe God has changed or that sin is any less crippling than it was in previous generations. But neither do I find that attempting to pin people to the wall with a personal condemnation which tries to awaken their guilt is going to help you persuade them to commit their lives to Christ. They will consider you some kind of oddball who is trying to gain relief at drawing other people into a guilt trip with you. I find it much better to allow the Holy Spirit to deal with that aspect of their relationship with God unless one of your friends brings it up himself. When that happens, you can then feel free to tell him about the forgiveness of sins inherent in a commitment of his life to Christ.

Most of the time I find that showing people how Christ can give them peace and power to make life come out right is the most effective thing I can do. That draws people like a magnet, while condemning them is a sure sign of spiritual immaturity, or worse, a neurotic desire to appear superior at the expense of others. There is no love in that, and since people can readily interpret such nonverbal communication, they will shun someone who does this like the plague, and with good reason. What he is offering is not the gospel of Christ, regardless of how he appropriates religious phrases to conceal his true motivation.

As a true witness, refuse to be drawn into unprofitable theological or psychological speculations. Your task is to tell what you have learned about the personal relationship one can have with Christ. Men and women from all denominations and classes of life, from the President of the United States to humble men and women in every city and town of the nation, are testifying that God does make their lives more complete and satisfying. Your task, in obeying the great commission of our Lord, is to focus on the problems people face and teach them how to find relief and fulfillment.

KEY CONCEPTS FROM CHAPTER SEVEN

1. When witnessing, anticipate the following questions:
   Will my acceptance of Christ do for me what you say it will?
   Is this the best choice for my life?
   Will this decision help me for the rest of my life?
2. The SAB approach leads up to a choice. The approach includes:

Solution:     the committing of one's life to Christ.
Advantage:    how living in Christ will empower his life.
Benefit:      how he will feel about himself and others
              when a positive decision has been made.

KEY QUESTIONS TO ASK YOURSELF

1.  Is my presentation both supportive and believable?
2.  Do I anticipate his potential questions about my recommendation?
3.  Do my SAB examples have an authentic ring to them?
4.  Am I recommending a fulfilling, meaningful life in Christ, rather than focusing on the wickedness of my friend?

# Eight

# Maintaining
# Interpersonal Trust

As you deal with your friend out of love and concern for him, keep coming back to two key questions in your mind. Ask yourself, "How can I help this person overcome his fears and objections?" Also, "How can I demonstrate my loving support in such a way that the Holy Spirit can get through to him?" As you find answers to the questions, you will be much more effective in helping him make a wise decision about his life.

At different times, as his interests shift, you will have to move back and forth from relating, to recognizing, to recommending in order to keep your discussion moving in a consistent manner. I find that in most cases I need more than a single session to lead a friend to make a positive decision for Christ; so you should plan to invest as long as he requires, since I personally cannot think of anything more important you can do for him. You will have to remain involved in his life on the physical and psychological levels if you want him to take your spiritual concerns seriously, for these needs are as important to him as the third level, his spiritual life.

If a person resists your attempts to move him toward an immediate decision, do not panic and try to overwhelm his resistance with facts, logic, or Scripture. That may be what he expects you to do, much like many salespersons trying to force a sale. Rather, you should remain his spiritual counselor who is helping him view all the aspects of the choice to make his own decision (which he is going to do, regardless of what you say, if it is to be valid). If you feel a growing resentment or resistance, relax the conversation with an appropriate third-person story in which you tell about someone who found greater satisfaction with his life by committing it to Christ. Follow that with a feeling-oriented question which causes him to think clearly about himself.

Often, as I witness, I find that people have been hurt earlier in their lives by the Christians they know or by some segment of the church. It is not helpful for you to tell such a person he was wrong and that the church doesn't do such things. After all, he was there and felt the pain; you were not. I have found a better way to deal with expressed anger or disappointment. You can say something like this to help him get his feelings of resentment out in the open so they can be dealt with:

"I hear you saying that you and your family have had some bad experiences with people in the church. Is that what you're telling me? It is too bad that some people fail to be good examples of Christ and I'd like to have you tell me more about that. If you don't mind, help me understand your feelings about that a little better."

Such an offer is rarely made to another person. Most people in our society believe that feelings are not as important as facts, so they try to brush feelings aside. Your act of acceptance may be the first time anyone has freely offered to listen compassionately to his story about something that was painful about his childhood or adolescence. Here is a good method I have found you can use to organize your acceptance of another person's frustration and turn the situation to his advantage:

*The ASRAC Process*

Start, as I have suggested throughout *The Psychology of Witnessing,* by considering his feelings as legitimate as are your facts.

*Accept all of his feelings.* After all, they will not go away simply because you pretend they don't exist. Listen with your eyes, ears and backbone. Listen without interruption, rebuttal or defense, even if he criticizes your pastor, your church, God or your own mother. If you have to, silently offer a short prayer to give you the grace to keep your mouth shut, especially if you are a controller or an entertainer. Listen selectively, responsively and with your heart until he is fully talked out about the matter. Let your tone, your vocabulary and your body language be accepting of him as a person who feels pain—for it is real to him whether you understand it or not. If necessary, remind yourself that you are working for his soul and not your own ego satisfaction. This is not a time to have your feelings ruffled and refuse to give him the freedom of discussion that you would want for yourself.

*Share his feelings as best you can.* Admit your own disappointment with some people in the church also, and admit that you wish people were perfect. Unfortunately, the Lord has given us this treasure in earthen vessels, as the Scripture tells us. And some of the pots are a little cracked! But we must do our best, of course, despite our limitations and flaws. For instance, when I was pastoring, I had a group of status-oriented people who put a great deal of pressure on me because I developed a program for, and ran a bus to collect, poor children from a rural community. Perhaps your friend has been hurt by something like this, and he has no way of knowing that such people are Law-oriented rather than gospel-centered. As truthfully as you can, empathize deeply about the unfortunate events which have disappointed him in the past.

*Reflect your friend's feelings to help him accept new information.* Your friend has taken a stand as he told you about his reason for being dissatisfied with the church (or whatever he has discussed). This was important for him to do as a means of getting it out in the open. Now, however, he will not want to appear weak-willed or inconsistent in changing his ideas about the church. Therefore, you will have to help him change his mind, even after he is half convinced that you are right. Do that as soon as possible, for if he gets the idea that a contest of wills is taking place, you have lost him, at least for the time being. Reflect his feelings accurately by paraphrasing his words and emotions as you learned to do earlier. You can say:

"Let me see if I understand you better now. You say that you have little use for the church since people in your childhood humiliated your parents because they were poor and couldn't send you kids to Sunday school dressed as nicely as the other children? Is that what you're telling me turned you off about the church? I can surely understand how that would have been devastating to a sensitive child who expected Christians to be above such narrowness."

Your suspicion that only a handful of cruel children made fun of him because of his ragged clothes does not matter. We know that children do things like that even when gospel-centered adults of a church would not dream of hurting the feelings of a child. His feelings are real to him, however, and should be taken seriously if you want to successfully witness to him. *Never*, therefore, devalue the importance of his feelings or contradict his feelings with your "facts" at this time. Doing so will surely put you in the same category as the people who made him feel bad in the past. If you tried to tell me that my feelings were not important, I would turn you away myself and consider you insensitive. And I would probably be right! Do, however, examine his emotions carefully with the paraphrase method so he will be able to see his feelings in perspective now that he is an adult.

*Add new facts to give him a logical reason to change his mind.* After you have used the reflection step to help him shift his frame of reference, adding new facts will allow him to consider your suggestions without appearing to be vacillating. These facts may be the same ideas you have previously discussed, but by repeating them at this step in the ASRAC process *in a new way*, you are giving him the logical reason he needs to appear consistent to himself. It is important to keep from appearing to argue or offer a challenge. Simply say something like this:

"I know that such things happen in the church, and I deeply regret it. Fortunately, in most churches, such things have changed. Most people now see how unimportant such surface things really are. Last Sunday in my own congregation I saw many men dressed quite casually. In fact, my own son wore a pair of corduroy trousers and a vest over a long-sleeved shirt. We are putting such things into better perspective than the church did years ago.

"In fact, it seems to me that the church really needs people like you to help us see how wrong we were in the past. We need you to help us become sensitive to our mistakes. Fortunately, Christ never treated people shabbily. Jesus accepted the kids of his day, even those running the streets, forbidding his followers from chasing them away. He was as much at home with Matthew the tax collector as he was with Joseph the Rabbi. We have a real need in the church for the sensitivity you could bring to us."

*Confirm his agreement to close the issue.* Your responsibility in this matter is neither to protect your ego nor to win an argument. It is to become the best witness of the love and mercy of Christ that you can be. Therefore, to return to the point you know to be crucial, close the side issue by asking for his confirmation that it is no longer important. You might say something like:

"I know that such things happen and they do leave people bitter; but knowing that Christ didn't reject anyone, and that the churches are trying to change, can I ask you to forgive our Christian insensitivity from your childhood? I'd like to ask your forgiveness for the entire church right now. Can I have it?"

It would be a rare man or woman who did not respond acceptingly to such an appeal from a person who is becoming a friend. Then you can go on to the central issue, which is the commitment of his life to Christ.

In the ASRAC process, *accepting, sharing,* and *reflecting* are means of dealing with feelings about issues which trouble him. They are in the same category as the feeling-oriented questions discussed earlier. *Adding* and *confirming* are intended to reach his adult ability to look at facts and solve problems. By using the five steps in sequence, you can deal more effectively with fear and objections. Actually, this is not only helpful but also critical, since few people are led to Christ without some problems and objections arising to block the successful conclusion of their accepting your invitation.

*Anxieties and Doubts*

Most refusals to make a Christian commitment as the divine integrating factor in life spring from fears of one kind or another. People frequently fear that Christ will not mean to them what you claim he will. Others resist making a decision for they suspect God will make demands on them which they are not willing to follow. Some fear they will become too dependent upon the church and other people, and they want to remain self-directing. I could go on with a long list of reasons people fear committing their lives to the Lord Jesus Christ; but the fact is that I find most refusals can be summed up in three basic categories, regardless of how they are stated. Underneath the window dressing I find that most people hesitate because:

1. *They have no faith in the witness or in religion as they learned it or as they saw it practiced by other people.*

2. *They have no need for a personal atonement, for they have not recognized the evil of sin, the inhumanity of man in his natural state, or the source of their unhappiness as alienation from God.*

3. *They have no commitment to anything beyond their own pleasure, power, or prestige, so they do not want to pay the price that being in Christ exacts from all believers.*

It is important for you to realize that virtually all refusals are based on ignorance, fear, or selfishness. Obviously, you do not tell this to your friend. This would imply that he is ignorant, fearful, or selfish. But you may be forced to exercise what I call tough love, in which your concern and compassion cause you to demand that he do what is best for himself rather than allow him to go on in mediocrity. Naturally, that would occur later in the relationship after the friendship has been well established. You should keep in mind the reasons for rejection as you plan your witness, however.

The person who has *no faith* is doubting your testimony for any number of reasons, most of which have nothing to do with you if you have related warmly and lovingly to him. Perhaps you caught him at a time when he had many other things on his mind. He may have accepted the atheistic, mechanistic concepts of life and matter which are taught in virtually all universities. Or he may be a practicing skeptic when things are going well for him and a "crisis Christian" when they are not. Then, too, he may believe that Jesus was only a superb moral teacher or a natural psychologist. But in any case, he does not believe your statements about Christ's ability to revolutionize a person's life.

An individual who does not yet see *his personal need* for Christ may require additional time for the Holy Spirit to apply your concern and words to him. In that case you must trust the Spirit enough to await his leading and plan to return later. Rome was not built in a day, and not all fruit ripens at the same time. In addition to that, some of the most competent Christian disciples I know are men and women who carefully thought through the ramifications of their personal commitment in advance. When they were finally convinced of their need and the fact that Christ does, indeed, offer a full restoration, they went all the way with him.

The third reason for hesitation to commit one's life to Christ is often based on the realization that *a price must be paid* in becoming a disciple. Compared to the costs of not following him, the price is light and easily paid. It often takes people a long time to discover this, however, unless some friend, because of his love, refuses to be turned away and continues to witness about the joy and deliverance to be gained in following Christ. People have to commit their careers, their friendships, their entertainments—everything—in a reversal of their entire life style. Perceptive but selfish people may see all this, acknowledge the truth of Christ's sacrifice, and still not be willing to pay the personal price involved.

Of course, as Christians, we recognize theirs is a short-sighted, self-crippling view; but it is one I encounter frequently in witnessing. Just recently, a young man I care deeply about told me that he couldn't live the Christian life because of his love of music. He said that should he follow Christ's command, he would have to stop playing in a rock music band. He said, "I'd have to give up everything I've studied for three years and play your old music, the kind Lawrence Welk plays."

Of course the Holy Spirit may have been convicting him about other things of which I had no knowledge, but his argument was a shallow one. I tried to tell him that the church offers many opportunities for a talented musician and that most Christian kids I know do not like the music my generation does, either. In fact, contemporary gospel music would shock the old European masters who composed and played music which was suited for their time and place in the church. I find in witnessing, as in my own life, that most of the barriers we perceive in our lives turn out to be blessings in disguise as we mature a little more.

Most people who have a fixation about not being able to live up to God's requirements are like a mule my grandfather had on the farm in Louisiana. That poor animal would not pass a certain burned-out, hollow cottonwood tree without throwing a fit. When we would get close to the tree, he would move more and more slowly. I would have to yell at him and whip him up to a run, or he would balk completely and try to go out in the field to get by. I walked by that tree twice every day for a whole summer one year and *never* did see what frightened Old Red. I finally came to the conclusion that the mule was not afraid of *what was there* but of what he *thought was there!* And so it is with many people. They don't fear what actually happens in a relationship with God, but what they *think* will happen if they commit their lives to Christ.

## Coping with Objections

While allowing fruit to ripen at individual rates of speed, I don't mean to imply that you should offer a mild suggestion about Christ and then retreat in disorder for the Spirit to carry on alone. You can apply the practical skills needed to keep your friend on track as you discuss his needs with him. In fact, I find the ability to lovingly cope with objections and resistance is extremely valuable in becoming a soul-winner. As you testify, there are three key methods you will find invaluable, since virtually every person I've ever spoken to about his need for Christ offers objections of some kind. I frequently get the impression that to be won over without offering at least token resistance makes people feel they are being manipulated. I understand this in our age of so many demands on our time, talents and money. We all have to rely on our good judgment to selectively screen the obligations people would place on us for their personal reasons.

Be that as it may, a majority of people automatically resist new ideas for a while, if for no other reason than to assert their independence. Besides, you are interjecting a new item in their list of priorities, one whose validity must be tested, accepted, and fit into their schedules. Don't be surprised or dismayed because of objections, but use this section to plan how to cope with them as you continue to press your case.

The three key methods I find most effective in continuing to offer others a chance to commit themselves to Christ are:

1. *Convert the objection into a question, and answer the question.*

2. *Use the feel, felt, and found approach to objections.*

3. *Use the boomerang approach to make the objection the very reason the person should commit his life to Christ.*

When converting an objection into a question, soften it with understanding and empathy before rephrasing it to match the person's acknowledged feelings. Suppose a man tells you that his parents lived a good life without being committed Christians. You might handle his objection this way:

"Let me see if I understand you correctly. You say that you wonder why your life should be any different from your parents in regards to religion? You wonder why you should live differently from them in regard to making a personal commitment? Is that the question that bothers you?"

If he does agree that this troubles him, you have reached an interpersonal discovery which will allow you to recommend a specific idea for his consideration. You may relate something like this:

"Cathy Wilson encountered this very problem with her kids. She had grown up much as you did, with good parents who were themselves raised in a simpler age. But when she moved to the city, she found her own kids under such pressures and temptations that she saw the need for a more positive spiritual life. She committed her life to Christ and brought her children to church with her. They're doing much better now. Does this answer your question?"

If he does not agree with your question or its answer, continue to talk to him, asking questions until you have reached another interpersonal discovery, and then advocate another aspect of the gospel to him.

When you use the feel, felt and found method to deal with objections, say something like the following, assuming that the person has said the same thing about his parents. Remain supportive, of course.

"I understand how you *feel*, for my parents (or my wife's parents or my Uncle John) were not committed Christians. They lived an unfocused life as far as God was concerned. They must have *felt* pretty much as your parents do, that Christ and the church are OK for women and kids. Unfortunately they *found*, as the resilience and hopes of youth and middle age faded, that they were growing more unhappy as the problems of aging without spiritual support grew more pronounced. It is a grim business to become old and frustrated, especially when life could be much more joyful and satisfying in God's love. I would hate to see you miss out on the many blessings God gives to a Christian because you failed to commit your life to Christ, my friend."

The feel, felt and found approach does not devalue his feelings, but builds upon them and shows the logical consequences of his unthinking adherence to family tradition in an age when many traditions have lost their value.

The boomerang method makes the objection the very reason he should do as you ask. It works like this:

"I know that in the past many good people accepted a general Christian morality for their lives. And this lack of personal commitment has led to much of the alienation and frustration people feel today, perhaps to some frustration and unhappiness for yourself. Fortunately, with today's changes and the spiritual awakening now taking place, you have an opportunity to live above the pressures of life to an extent your parents did not understand. You can commit your life to Christ and have a depth of meaning and fulfillment that will make your life even fuller and more rewarding than your parents' lives have been, for as long as you live and beyond."

As you speak to his objections, do not try to use a canned refutation but probe for his feelings as you proceed. Continue to recognize what he is implying until you find the ideas which will prompt your friend to recognize his need for Christ, and then ask him to commit himself fully. Continue to ask questions which will keep him thinking seriously about the purpose of your visit, and be willing to let him speak his mind fully. Allowing him to talk rather than merely listen will not detract from the process, but gives both of you a better understanding of his needs and the solutions that being in Christ brings.

I have found a simple technique to use when answering objections or neutralizing resistance. When it is possible, I use the word *and* rather than *but* in refuting ideas. If a friend says he does not have time for religious matters and you say, "I understand that *but*. . . ," you have both contradicted him and devalued his feelings. You have also shown that you do not really understand life as he sees it, that his feelings are not clear to you. It is much better to say something like this:

"I understand how busy you are making a living, now that you and Jill are starting a family and your career is going so well. *And* I have found that living in Christ will help make things better, despite the time you must spend away from Jill and the kids. In fact, I have found that committing my life to Christ makes my life worth all the work I put into earning a living."

In this second example the friend has been accepted and his ideas have been considered, and *then* something has been added to them. You have demonstrated understanding and have not devalued his previous statement. When it is appropriate, use *and* instead of *but* in dealing with objections.

Obviously, this is an area in which you will have to be careful to remain supportive, yet honest, as you deal with the realities of life both *with and without* Christ. You will have to refute your friend's statements at times if you are to continue witnessing in such a way that he will listen to you. The only other alternative is giving up and letting him be. By learning to cope with the fears and objections which lie behind most refusals, you can become a much more effective witness for Christ.

KEY CONCEPTS FROM CHAPTER EIGHT

1.  The steps of the ASRAC process are:
    *Accept*
    *Share*
    *Reflect* . . . when dealing with feelings.
    *Add*
    *Confirm* . . . when dealing with facts.
2.  Three ways of dealing effectively with objections and resistance are:
    Convert objection to question and answer it.
    Use the feel, felt and found method.
    Use the boomerang approach.
3.  Use the word *and* rather than *but* as often as you can when contradicting a friend to whom you are witnessing.

KEY QUESTIONS TO ASK YOURSELF

1.  Have I anticipated any possible objections that can arise because of his personality pattern?

2. Have I practiced the ASRAC process until I am confident in using it?
3. Am I prepared to use the three methods of handling objections?
4. Do I frequently devalue people by saying "Yes, but . . ."?

# Nine

# Asking for a Decision

Virtually everything in this book has but one purpose—to help you become more effective in leading other people to make a commitment of their lives to Christ. Unfortunately, many Christians witness by telling others what the Lord has done for them without ever asking their friends to make a decision for Christ. I find that this hesitation in asking for a commitment comes from the anxiety people normally have about being rejected in something that is important to them. This anxiety is similar to that felt by a young man who loves a girl, wants to marry her, carries a ring for weeks, but still hesitates to propose because he is afraid of being refused. He hopes that she will sense his desire and get him off the hook without his becoming vulnerable to rejection.

Because we consciously and unconsciously want to avoid pain, we often protect ourselves by not asking our friends to make a clear-cut decision about the Lord. This is tragic—for if we really believe that Christ is the answer to the world's problems, we are doing our friend, society and God an injustice in putting our fears ahead of their needs. No doubt this anxiety is deepened by one's awkwardness in witnessing, but when one follows the Holy Spirit and learns to use the methods taught here, the fears will vanish. This will lead to more self-confidence as an increasing number of friends are led to a personal decision for Christ.

*The Importance of a Decision*

A personal decision to commit one's life to Christ is both psychologically and theologically valid. A mere mental acceptance of a concept (such as Jesus' sacrifice) need only be compared to an intense love relationship to understand the difference between acquiescing and committing. Twenty-eight years ago I committed my love to Roberta. I did not just accept her as a neat person with whom to while away a few hours. I fell deeply in love with her. She fully occupied my thoughts, my fantasies and my longings for a life together—becoming more important to me than any other person. I decided that I did not want to live apart from her, and since she felt the same way about me, we *committed* our lives to each other. More of our lives have been spent together now than the years we lived apart before we met. The commitment occurred at a specific time and place in our lives, though I cannot pinpoint the day I first realized I loved her.

I find that much the same thing takes place in making a commitment to Christ. A person may have a growing interest in spiritual matters and in learning more about the nature of a spiritual rebirth. In virtually all cases that I know anything about, however, a time and place can be identified when the individual seizes hold of the fact that he must commit his life, for better or worse, to Christ as Savior Generally, the exceptions to this have been people who grew up in spiritual homes where they made a commitment at such an early age that they cannot remember when it happened. Roberta is such a person. Her parents were such committed Christians that she grew up in an atmosphere of *agape* through which her commitment was made as she was learning how to sing her childhood songs about Jesus. I have little doubt that this is the best way a person's commitment could come about; but when it hasn't, each person needs, from both theological and psychological viewpoints, to make a conscious affirmation of his life to Christ.

*Clarifying the Decision*

Asking for a personal commitment can be done in several ways, even when your friend has proven hesitant earlier. In few instances will a refusal be directed at you personally if you have earned the right to recommend a solution to his perceived problems. It will most likely be the result of his fear or confusion about what you are asking him to do. If this is the case, you will never know unless you provide your friend with additional opportunities to choose Christ. You will have to plan to come back after you have prepared for another visit. Since the Holy Spirit always deals fairly with an honest seeker who is sincerely trying to sort out his feelings and needs, remain patient as you do your part in the work God has given us all.

You certainly should not think of yourself as being a failure if your friend has not done as you asked. After all, losing a single opportunity for the time being is not in the same category as failing to accept Christ's commission to witness! As your skills improve and the relationship with your friend deepens, you can visit with him and try once more to lead your friend to Christ. Remember that he has an even deeper fear of acting foolishly than your fear of rejection or failure. You know that what you're doing is for the best, even if you are not satisfied with your own skills at the time. He may be concerned that he will look foolish to his spouse, relatives and friends. His fears are not entirely unjustified, for consider how Chuck Colson's friends reacted when he committed his life to Christ. They were quick with their ridicule and criticism. They snickered that the pressure was getting to him and he was cracking up.

If you feel your friend is afraid of making a mistake or looking foolish, take special pains to assure him that people in all walks of life are taking the same step as the tide of relational Christianity mounts even higher. Take time to listen to what he is *not* saying as well as to what he is saying. If you meet reluctance to go any further, pause and help him discover his needs and reasons for wanting Christ's help in his life. Re-enter the discovery phase once more and rebuild the interpersonal discovery with him before continuing to advocate a solution.

I always try to think positively from the beginning and assume that the Holy Spirit knew what he was doing when he led me to speak to my friend about Christ. With that faith, I do the following:

*Believe*
*Clarify*
*Confirm*

*Believe* that your friend is intelligent enough to see the importance of ending the spiritual bankruptcy of his life by making the best choice God has available for him. After all, your friend can see his needs, the potential benefits of living a Christian life, and the sad results of not living a spiritual existence as you witnessed truthfully to him. As you assume that he is going to choose wisely, you can try a minor decision on him at first. Ask him if he would like you to offer a prayer for wisdom as he makes up his mind. If he agrees, telling you to pray, you know that he will soon be ready for another decision of even greater importance.

You should also *clarify* what you are asking him to do. Don't be like the student minister I heard speak recently. Afterwards, when a friend and I walked out of the sanctuary, my friend leaned over toward me and whispered, "Andy is very persuasive, isn't he? I feel like I should go out and do something, but for the life of me, I can't figure out what it is!"

Point out what will happen if he trusts Christ as his personal Savior, as opposed to what will happen if he does not. Be supportive, but honest, at this point. Clarify the issue still further by asking which of the benefits you have discussed would be most important to him should he commit his life to Christ. Tell him about some happy event experienced by someone you know who committed his life to Christ recently.

A third-party example here, rather than talking about your own experiences, will broaden the scope of his expectations. You can clarify the value that being a Christian will have for him by telling him what kind of things will happen immediately if he will make his decision right away. You can simply say, "If you made such a commitment of your life today, you would have the weekend to share your new faith with your family." It does not have to be profound, simply something to look forward to as a means of focusing his attention on an immediate decision. You could also say:

"Life involves so many chance happenings that you

should take care of your spiritual well-being right now. Make your commitment today, John, and you will have your entire vacation to discover how to gain the most peace and fulfillment from your new-found relationship with God."

There are times when you may have to become like the faithful family physician who exercises tough love with his patients who are injuring their health. When you do this, challenging your friend in no-nonsense terms, you will especially need the leading of the Holy Spirit. In fact, I cannot believe that he will lead you to use it until you have been faithful as a friend, discovered his needs, and talked to him many times about his spiritual health. With your tone and body language still expressing love and support, you might have to say something like the following:

"Sally, I love you too much to see you go on in such confusion and pain any longer. You need to screw your head on straight and stop deceiving yourself! You cannot live a Christian life and hang on to the kind of relationships you keep. They are tearing you apart.

"Let's kneel right here by your table as you offer your life to Christ! I care too much about you to remain silent any longer while you drift from man to man, as you have been doing since your divorce. Come and kneel with me right now as I pray, and then *you* pray a prayer for committal for your life. Come, kneel with me, Sally!"

This can be the final push some people need; but you must be sensitive to the situation, your standing with your friend, and especially the leading of the Spirit at the time. A mistake could ruin the relationship you have built up over a period of time.

Finally, *confirm* the other person's decision by summarizing the facts he has to weigh. List the facts and feelings the two of you have discussed, but remember that you are not making a sales pitch. It is the conclusion of a discussion with a friend in which you are helping him discover his needs and find a solution which is effective now and in the future because you sincerely love him. Make sure you are relating to him with visible love by demonstrating acceptance, understanding and involvement.

A person who is ready to make a serious decision about any aspect of life will send out nonverbal signals before he tells you about it verbally. He may respond with excitement or a forward movement of his body toward the speaker. He may make an accepting gesture, such as turning his palm upward or nodding. He may make a specific, positive statement about the Christian life, about his need for spiritual guidance, or about the responsible choices a man or woman in Christ has to make.

When you see such a sign, stop there and ask him to commit his life to Christ on the spot! In his mind he is doing what you ask, so go ahead and ask him. You can say something like:

"Why don't we stop right now and pray a prayer of committal for your life? Would you prefer that I pray first, or would you want to?"

Or, "I realize that you see the importance of such a spiritual decision about your life. Take that step with me now. We can pray right here. Would you rather we knelt together, or would you prefer we stayed in our chairs as you pray a prayer of commitment to Christ?"

Offering an option, like the place of prayer, shows him that you are still concerned more about his needs than in having your own way. It also reveals to you that he has made a positive decision as he chooses one place or the other. Besides, as every salesman knows, offering a choice is always more successful than a blunt "Will you or won't you?" challenge.

I must caution you, however. You must not, in any way, make the commitment for him. You can witness, advocate, pray and persuade, but the commitment to Christ and the prayer of dedication must always remain his own. The act of closure has a psychological benefit as well as a spiritual one. It can keep the issue from coming up again at a time of doubt. He can point to the specific time and place and recall what actually happened and thus maintain his confidence.

The prayer should contain whatever he wants to put into it. You are not with him to instruct him in the act of prayer, but to guide his commitment. If he wants to ask forgiveness for sins, to commit his money and time, to make restitution for past wrongs, go ahead and accept his prayer with him. If he wants to do that privately, this remains between himself and God. It is beyond your responsibility.

When your friend has made his commitment, spend some time rejoicing with him and assuring him that he has done the right thing. Pray with him and make arrangements to give all possible support in the crucial weeks that lie ahead. Work hard to get your friend involved in the church and committed to its work. See that other friends know about his choice and stand by him with the acceptance and support he needs in such a time of self-examination. Throughout the entire process, continue to be his friend and help him mature in Christ every way you can as you teach him to become a better Christian.

I know of no greater joy than that of leading another person to Christ, and I have found no better way of doing that successfully than the way described in *The Psychology of Witnessing*. Apply the methods and techniques, but feel free to modify them in any way which makes you more successful in following the commission of Jesus. Use them according to your own personality pattern traits and interests, and according to your own creative imagination.

Above all, remember that it is the Holy Spirit's work to convict and convince of sin. It is our responsibility to be available and willing to be used of the Spirit according to his leading. Old J. R. Miller (1840–1912) put it well when he wrote:

> We must love those we seek to save, but we must love Christ more; we must love them because we love Christ, because he loves them, because he gave himself for them. We must strive to win souls, not for ourselves, but for Christ. It is not enough to get people to love us; we must get them to love our Saviour, to trust in him, and to commit their lives to him. We must hide ourselves away out of sight. He who is thinking of his own honour as he engages in any Christian service is not a vessel ready to be used by Christ. We need to take care that no shadows of ourselves, of our pride, our ambition, our self-seeking, fall upon our work for Christ.

KEY CONCEPTS FROM CHAPTER NINE

1. Many Christians fail to witness well because they fear rejection.
2. A refusal of commitment to Christ is rarely directed at you personally.
3. In drawing the visit to a decision, *believe* that your friend will see his needs, *clarify* the implications, and *confirm* the benefits with him.
4. Ask for a decision for Christ when you see by his nonverbal signals that he is ready to do so.

KEY QUESTIONS TO ASK YOURSELF

1. Have you earned the right to ask your friend to make a decision by spending time, prayer and study in recognizing his needs?

2.  Have you sincerely believed that the Holy Spirit is going to lead both of you?
3.  Do you watch for nonverbal signals of acceptance?
4.  Have you cleared out the underbrush of analogy and euphemisms so there is no chance for him to mistake what you are asking him to do?
5.  Have you given him a choice which will enable him to pray a prayer of acceptance?

Believe ⎫
Clarify ⎬ p. 120
Confirm ⎭

Relate in love & Compassion ⎞
Recognize how he sees his needs ⎬ p. 19
Recommend a Sensible Solution ⎠

"I would rather be robbed every second Thursday.
p. 65/

The mule "Ol Red" threw a fit every time he
had to walk by a certain stump. p. 110